PROMO 2

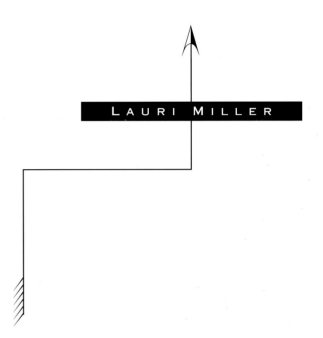

LAURI MILLER

THE ULTIMATE IN
GRAPHIC DESIGNER'S
AND ILLUSTRATOR'S
SELF-PROMOTION

NORTH
LIGHT
BOOKS

CINCINNATI, OHIO

96   95   5   4

Library of Congress Cataloging-in-Publication Data

Promo 2 : the ultimate in graphic designer's and illustrator's self-promotion /
     [compiled by] Lauri Miller.
          p.   cm.
     ISBN 0-89134-451-9
     1. Graphic arts — United States — Marketing.   2. Graphic arts — United
States — Management.   3. Communication in design.
I. Miller, Lauri.   II. Title: Promo two.
NC998.5.A1P76 1992
741.6'068'8 — dc20   92-10735
                                                  CIP

Edited by Diana Martin and Kathy Kipp
Designed by Sandy Conopeotis with David Betz

I WOULD LIKE TO THANK THE DESIGNERS,
ILLUSTRATORS AND PHOTOGRAPHERS WHOSE WORK
APPEARS HERE, WITHOUT WHOM THERE WOULD BE
NO BOOK; KATHY KIPP, FOR HER PLEASANT
DEMEANOR AND CONSTANT ENCOURAGEMENT; BETH
JOHNSON, FOR CAREFULLY SEEING THE BOOK
THROUGH PRODUCTION; AND KRISTI CULLEN, SANDY
CONOPEOTIS AND PAM MONFORT, FOR MAKING IT SO
LOVELY. AND THANKS, AS ALWAYS, TO CONNIE
ACHABEL, FOR HER UNDERSTANDING AND
UNFLAGGING SUPPORT.

ACKNOWLEDGMENTS

TO CLAY, MY WISE ONE.

DEDICATION

CONTENTS

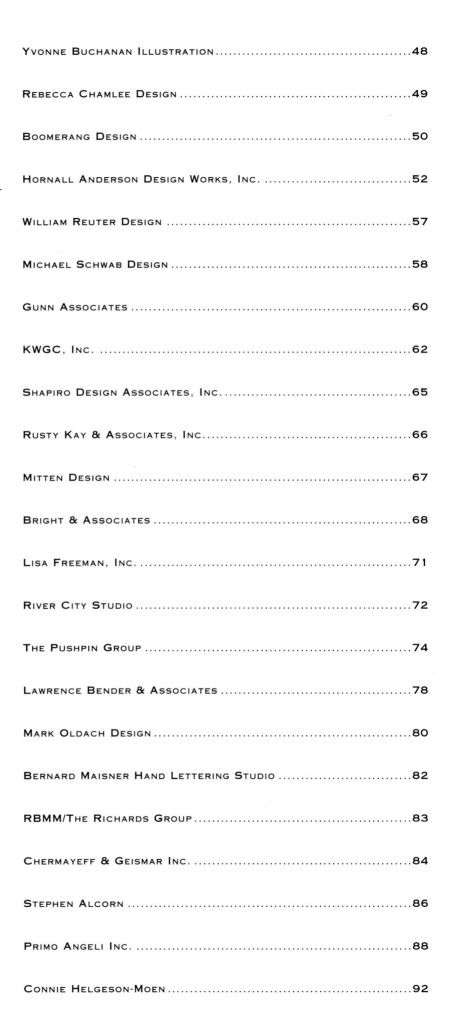

CONTENTS, CONTINUED

IN 1990 NORTH LIGHT BOOKS PUBLISHED <u>PROMO 1: THE ULTIMATE IN GRAPHIC DESIGNER'S AND ILLUSTRATOR'S SELF-PROMOTION</u>. A CLASS ACT IN ITSELF, IT ALSO SET THE STAGE FOR WHAT WOULD BECOME A NORTH LIGHT TRADITION. NOW WE PRESENT <u>PROMO 2</u>, A SHOWCASE OF RECENT PROMOTIONAL WORK DONE BY TODAY'S MOST CREATIVE AND INNOVATIVE DESIGNERS, ILLUSTRATORS AND PHOTOGRAPHERS. IT IS WORK THAT WAS CLEARLY CONCEIVED, WELL-DESIGNED, APPROPRIATE TO ITS AUDIENCE, AND SUCCESSFUL IN ACHIEVING ITS GOALS.

AS THIS COLLECTION ILLUSTRATES, SUCCESSFUL PROMOTION DOESN'T INVOLVE GIMMICK AND INSINCERITY; NOR DOES IT HAVE TO BE AN ENERVATING TASK. IT CAN (AND SHOULD) BE A TRUE EXPRESSION OF ONE'S WORK AND ONE'S OFFERINGS, CRAFTED WITH TENDERNESS AND CARE. IT CAN BE A REFRESHING CHANCE TO FLEX THE CREATIVE MUSCLE, FOR THERE ARE NO LIMITS TO WHAT PROMOTION CAN BE.

<u>PROMO 2</u> PRESENTS AN EVEN MORE ECLECTIC MIX OF PROMOTIONAL WORK THAN DID ITS PREDECESSOR BECAUSE IT HAS BEEN OPENED UP TO INCLUDE CLIENT PROMOTIONS AS WELL AS SELF-PROMOTIONS. EVERYTHING FROM A MAGAZINE MEDIA KIT AND CORPORATE ANNUAL REPORT TO A PRO BONO THEATRE POSTER AND SOCIAL SERVICE ORGANIZATION BROCHURE TO A SELF-PROMOTIONAL CALENDAR AND HOLIDAY CARD ARE INCLUDED AMONG THESE PAGES.

WHILE SOME OF THESE PROMOTIONS WERE LAVISHLY PRODUCED, A GREAT MANY HAD LOW BUDGETS, REFLECTING THE TENOR OF THE RECESSIONARY TIME IN WHICH THEY WERE CREATED. MANY PIECES IN THIS BOOK WERE REALIZED THROUGH TRADE WITH PRINTERS, PAPER COMPANIES AND OTHER SUPPLIERS; COST-CUTTING PRODUCTION TECHNIQUES, SUCH AS HAND-STAMPS AND MANUAL DIE-CUTS; AND THE USE OF MATERIALS RECYCLED FROM OTHER PROJECTS.

ALTHOUGH EACH PROMOTION IN <u>PROMO 2</u> IS UNIQUE, THERE ARE CERTAIN CONCERNS AND APPROACHES THAT RECUR. FOR ONE, THERE IS AN ECONOMIC PRUDENCE, WHICH DOES NOT MEAN THEY WERE BORNE OF CAUTION, BUT RATHER THAT THEY WERE PLANNED AND EXECUTED ECONOMICALLY, WITH THE INTENTION THAT THEY WOULD LIVE LONG LIVES AND STAY OUT OF THEIR RECIPIENTS' WASTEBASKETS. GONE, FOR

THE MOST PART, ARE PROMOTIONS THAT DO NOT FIT IN A FILE DRAWER OR SERVE A FUNCTION.

BOOKS ARE HARD TO PART WITH, AND THROWING OUT A BOOK, HOWEVER SMALL, IS DIFFICULT TO DO, WHICH MAY EXPLAIN WHY BOOKLETS HAVE ACHIEVED SUCH POPULARITY. ITS PREVALENCE MAY ALSO POINT TO A QUIET RECELEBRATION OF THE HANDMADE AND TACTILE AESTHETIC OF THE DESIGN OF YESTERDAY, IN CONTRAST TO THE HIGH-TECH COMPUTER AESTHETIC OF TODAY. THESE BOOKS ARE OFTEN COLLATED BY HAND, WITH UNUSUAL BINDINGS—TWIGS, NAILS, BITS OF STRAW OR RIBBON. THE PAPER IS SOMETIMES HANDMADE, OFTEN RECYCLED.

CONCERN FOR THE ENVIRONMENT IS SEEN THROUGHOUT. THREE-DIMENSIONAL (INCLUDING EDIBLE) GIFTS HAVE BECOME TREE SEEDLINGS, BANNERS THAT APPEAL TO LOCAL COMMUNITIES TO RECYCLE THEIR CHRISTMAS TREES, AND NOTICE OF THE FACT THAT TREES HAVE BEEN PLANTED IN CLIENTS' NAMES.

GREAT ATTENTION IS PAID TO SOCIAL AND POLITICAL ISSUES: A RESPONSE TO AIDS, HOMELESSNESS, RACIAL TENSIONS, AND INFRINGEMENTS ON FREEDOM OF SPEECH. WHILE THESE CONCERNS ARE MOST OFTEN SEEN IN PRO BONO AND SELF-PROMOTIONAL WORK, THEY SOMETIMES FIND THEIR WAY INTO CLIENT PROMOTIONS AS WELL, EXEMPLIFIED BY BERNHARDT FUDYMA'S HIGHLY ORIGINAL PROMOTION FOR GILBERT PAPER.

WHAT ALL OF THESE PIECES HAVE IN COMMON IS THE IMMENSE AMOUNT OF TALENT AND CREATIVITY THAT WENT INTO THEM; THE DISCIPLINE THAT WAS REQUIRED TO MOVE THEM FROM CONCEPT TO PRODUCT; AND THE PERSISTENCE INVOLVED IN MAKING THEM A SUCCESS BY FOLLOWING UP AFTER THEY WERE MAILED.

LONG HOURS AND HARD WORK WENT INTO THE PROMOTIONS SANDWICHED AMONG THESE PAGES. IT IS A HEARTY FILLING, WHICH, IT IS HOPED, WILL TEACH, INSPIRE AND TRIGGER YOUR IMAGINATIONS—AS THE FIRST STEP IN SUCCESSFULLY PROMOTING YOURSELF.

—LAURI MILLER

There is whimsy and charm in Steven Guarnaccia's illustration, as well as an intelligence and angularity of form. One senses that for Guarnaccia there must be an almost immediate release of his imagination into his art, and there is—in his doodles. Guarnaccia was granted the chance to bring his doodles directly to his editorial illustration for B.W. Honeycutt, art director of *Spy*, in developing the "I Spy" series for the magazine. What emerged, says Guarnaccia, was "a new way of working, the development of a new style." He was then able to inexpensively turn the series into a self-promotion through trade with the lithographer D.L. Terwilliger/Sterling Roman, for whom he designed the Season's Greeting card on page six.

Two thousand of each of the four-color "I Spy" postcards showcasing a series Guarnaccia did for Spy magazine were "haphazardly" distributed to his clients.

To engage the reader while announcing a show of his work, Guarnaccia cleverly created this highly original, letterpressed mailer entitled "Paperwork." It was sent to those on Reactor Gallery's list, clients, family and friends.

This Physicians Health Service brochure, entitled "Survival Guide," and mailed to members of HMOs, offers fun, educational and inspirational information on how to be healthy—stay alive and live well. "Rules of Thumb" appeals to the intellect; "Fieldwork" leads to action; and "Health Stamps" passes the word on.

When American Illustration Nine *and* American Photography Six *were published, American Illustration, Inc. decided to throw a party, a black-and-white-plus-one-color party. Who could resist going when Guarnaccia so happily and elegantly conveys how much fun it could be!*

Designed and illustrated by Guarnaccia for D.L. Terwilliger/ Sterling Roman in exchange for the printing of his "I Spy" cards, this Season's Greeting card conveys the glee of being bundled up and shopping along city streets during the holiday season.

The Christmas following the outbreak of war in the Persian Gulf impelled many to reflect on the human condition and cry out for world peace, including the staff of Morla Design. Kind to the earth in the process, the graphic design, interior architecture and signage team simply presented their message on three pieces of foil-stamped chipboard, utilizing the envelope die from their 1989 Christmas card. The important message is directly and powerfully conveyed by combining symbols of the earth, the peace sign, and the word "Peace" in five languages with their unique alphabets: Hebrew, Greek, Chinese, Russian and Farsi. Five hundred went out to clients, suppliers and friends at a cost of five dollars apiece. The card struck a chord with many, for the design studio received hundreds of calls in response.

The design, layout and type of this three-piece card were computer-generated, output to Linotronic. It was offset printed in two color and foil-stamped; money was saved due to the small size of the foil-stamping area and the fact that it was partially donated by a die company.

Twenty-five hundred of these brochures were produced at an estimated cost of $3,500 to $4,000. Three match colors and varnish, computer-generated type and offset printing were employed to create this good-looking and informative brochure.

The Nabisco logo is an enigmatic one, offering no hint as to the whys of its design. Originally created in 1900, the logo was redesigned by the Bernhardt Fudyma Design Group in 1990, for the first time in more than thirty years. Once the project was completed, the firm wished to share both their accomplishment and their newfound knowledge of how an ancient symbol, the shape of a cracker and an innovative packaging technique contributed to the trademark's evolution. So they created this richly designed accordion-fold brochure. Distributed in one initial mailing, its subtle communication of the firm's capabilities also makes it an effective leave-behind.

"You Can't Say That" is the firm's contribution to Gilbert Paper's annual "Designer Potpourri," the theme of which was "Freedom of Expression." Due to the events of the time, says Craig Bernhardt, "the Mapplethorpe trial, the debate over flag burning, the censoring of recordings, etc.," the firm conceived this "obvious approach." They have received many calls as a result, while for Gilbert the response has been "immeasurable"—and continues even today.

In addition to expressing concerns about on-going attacks on freedom of speech, this spiral-bound, seven-color booklet shows the thoughtful and visually arresting aspect of Bernhardt Fudyma's design. And for the client, Gilbert Paper, it creatively conveys to the design and printing communities the printability and versatility of two of their many papers. Forty thousand were produced at a cost of $35,000.

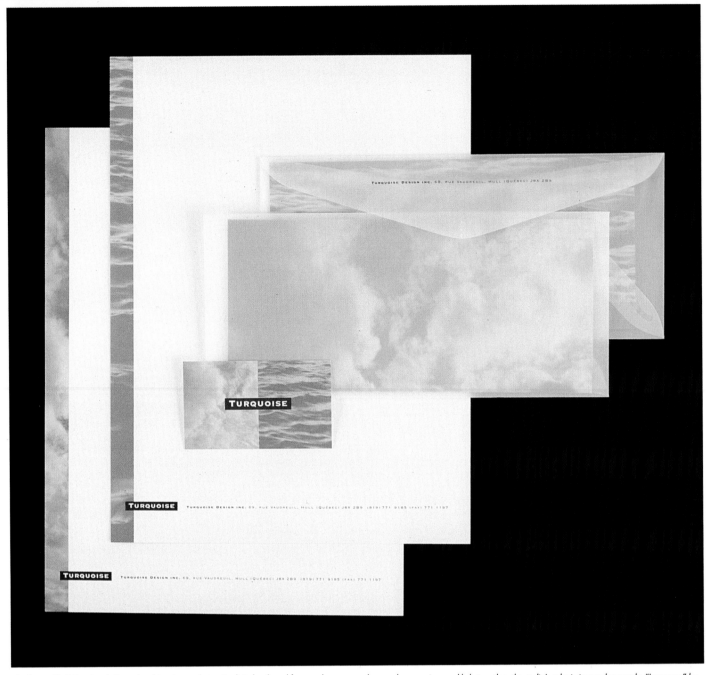

Art director Mark Timmings believes that this unique and attractive letterhead, used for everyday correspondence and communiques, added strength to the studio's submissions and proposals. "I am sure," he says, "that some of the hard-to-get clients may have called us back after receiving the letter, in part, because they were impressed by the stationery." The design and layout to camera-ready artwork was done in-house.

To mark their tenth anniversary, Turquoise Design created new corporate identity and stationery that pulls together the firm's unique characteristics: the qualities of the mineral of their namesake, the natural environment of their location, and the new technology of their workplace. Just as turquoise is blue, bluish green and greenish grey, so too is their letterhead. While the back of one is printed with a ghostly sky photograph of blue, the back of the other presents a water photograph of green. Juxtaposed with this expression of environmental sensitivity is computer-designed typography, representing the firm's active response to technology. "We wanted to create a sense of depth and unique tactile quality by incorporating translucent material for the envelope," says art director Mark Timmings. The challenge, he says, "was finding a supplier for the envelope in North America. After several unsuccessful attempts at folding and gluing, we approached a European manufacturer who produced the envelopes promptly and economically." The production cost totalled $10,390 in Canadian dollars for three thousand copies of each item.

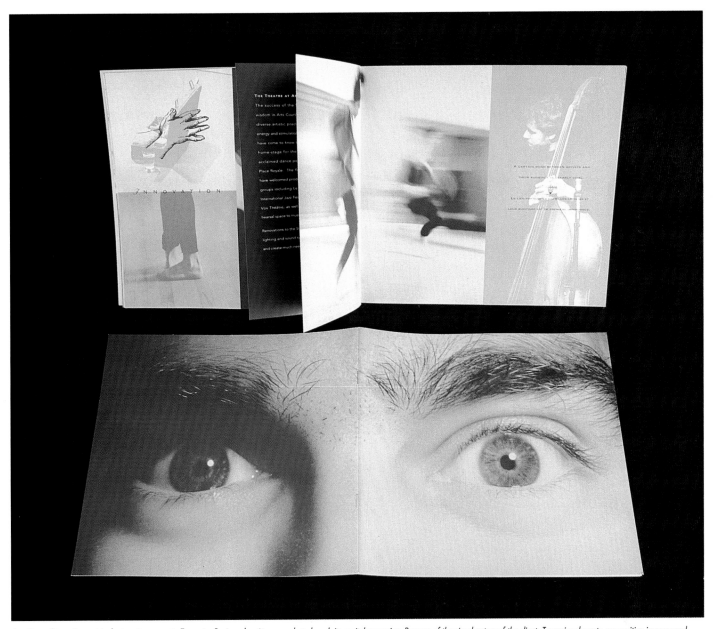

Arts Court, Ottawa's municipal art center, came to Turquoise Design when it was ready to launch its capital campaign. Because of the visual nature of the client, Turquoise chose to use exciting imagery and "tell the whole story in pictures," says art director Mark Timmings. For one thousand copies the total production cost was $13,750 in Canadian dollars. The brochure is visually impressive without being lavish. "Cultural clients don't often have big bucks," says Timmings, "and during a fund raising campaign isn't a great time to look rich."

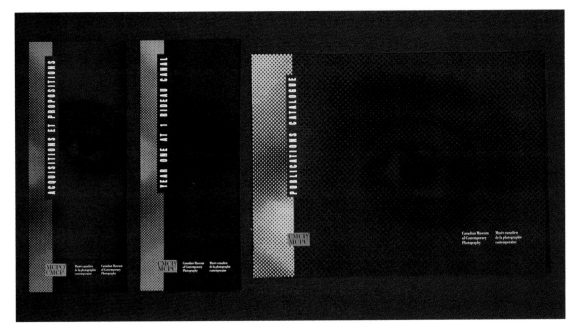

To package information for and promote interest in the Canadian Museum of Contemporary Photography, designer Daniel Lohnes established, he says, "a contemporary identity that represents the different aspects of photography, both aesthetic and technical." For five thousand of the publication catalog, twenty-five hundred copies of the acquisitions pamphlet, and twenty thousand copies of the general information pamphlet, the cost was $40,000 in Canadian dollars.

When the designers at Ultimo Inc., headed by Clare Ultimo, make a statement that shares their philosophy, they try do so without doing a preachy superiority dance. For example, to address the interdependence of their and their client's actions and take responsibility for the amount of paper they use, the studio donated money to the Sempervirens Fund in California to have trees planted in honor of their clients. "Little" trees were then given to serve as an everyday reminder of the depletion of this natural resource. The gift went out to ninety-eight clients and cost approximately $1,600. The holiday card that year had the same natural look and feel. The 5 1/2" x 8 1/2" piece consisted of two sheets of a nonplastic type vellum. Underneath the two-color image were fresh pine needles, which gave the cards a festive and fresh scent. At least ten to fifteen clients and friends, Ultimo says, "called to say they were moved when they received it." Both the tree-planting project and the card were intended to raise consciousness, but also raised revenue: The studio received a renewal contract with an environmental group they weren't expecting due to budget cuts.

Money was saved by printing both tree gift tags and holiday greeting cards at the same time using the same papers and colors. "We bought cheap 'take-out' brown paper bags," says Clare Ultimo, "and stamped our company logo on them and the tissue by hand. It was a cheap way to personalize our packaging."

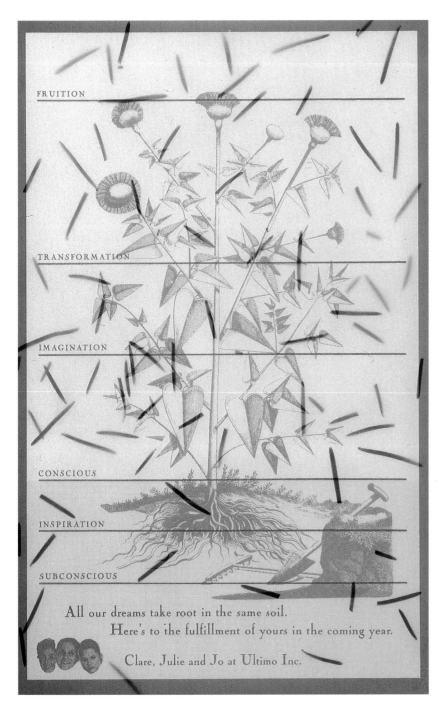

FRUITION

TRANSFORMATION

IMAGINATION

CONSCIOUS

INSPIRATION

SUBCONSCIOUS

All our dreams take root in the same soil.
Here's to the fulfillment of yours in the coming year.

Clare, Julie and Jo at Ultimo Inc.

Ultimo Inc. spends anywhere from $6,000 to $8,000 annually on self-promotion. Two hundred fifty copies of this holiday greeting card were produced for $500. "We wanted to remind all our friends and clients that dreams, indeed, can become reality," explains Clare Ultimo. Cards were folded by hand after they were filled with fresh pine needles.

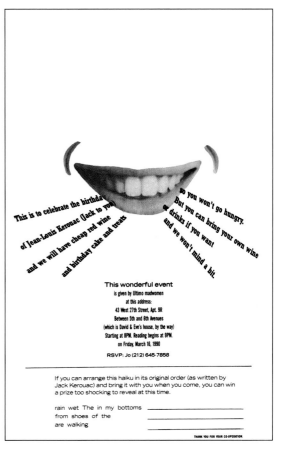

This is to celebrate the birthday of Jean-Louis Kerouac (Jack to you) and we will have cheap red wine and birthday cake and treats so you won't go hungry. But you can bring your own wine or drinks if you want and we won't mind a bit.

This wonderful event
is given by Ultimo madwomen
at this address:
43 West 27th Street, Apt. 9R
Between 5th and 6th Avenues
(which is David & Eve's house, by the way)
Starting at 8PM. Reading begins at 9PM.
on Friday, March 16, 1990

RSVP: Jo (212) 645-7858

If you can arrange this haiku in its original order (as written by Jack Kerouac) and bring it with you when you come, you can win a prize too shocking to reveal at this time.

rain wet The in my bottoms
from shoes of the
are walking

THANK YOU FOR YOUR CO-OPERATION.

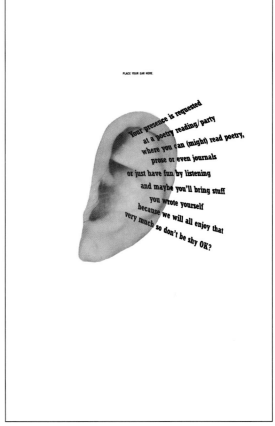

PLACE YOUR EAR HERE.

Your presence is requested at a poetry reading/party where you can (might) read poetry, prose or even journals or just have fun by listening and maybe you'll bring stuff you wrote yourself because we will all enjoy that very much so don't be shy OK?

Poetry reading invitation in honor of Jack Kerouac's birthday. Two hundred fifty were produced for about $350. The inspiration says Clare Ultimo, a former English major, was "a love of poetry and the Beats—a desire to make that more accessible to our clients and friends in a relaxed atmosphere of a party, much like the poetry readings of the fifties and sixties." The simple and direct design helped the studio acquire more creative (less corporate) work.

Hungry Dog's promotions are simple and inexpensive expressions of their impassioned illustration—a rush of color and primal imagery that dances and screams. To generate assignments in the recording industry, the team of Bob and Val Tillery developed the above promotion in which they visually interpreted their favorite songs. Enveloped sets of four cards were mailed out to various recording, entertainment, editorial, design and advertising markets throughout a two-year period with a handmade die-cut box as a final follow-up. The $650 venture showcases their power of interpretation and ability to handle likenesses and resulted in much album and CD cover work as well as entertainment-oriented editorial work. The 5" x 7" cards on the next page utilize personal themes and were sent to various advertising, editorial and design markets.

The studio is still receiving calls from the above promotion, intended to appeal primarily to the music industry. The "theme song" cards were color-photocopied and everything else was done by hand, including the red die-cut box they were mailed in.

One of three sets of laser-printed, color-photocopied, mounted and hand-stamped cards, featuring the work of both artists. It was inspired by the realization that "I can do whatever I want on a five- by seven-inch card," explains Val Tillery. Fifty sets were created at a cost of $300.

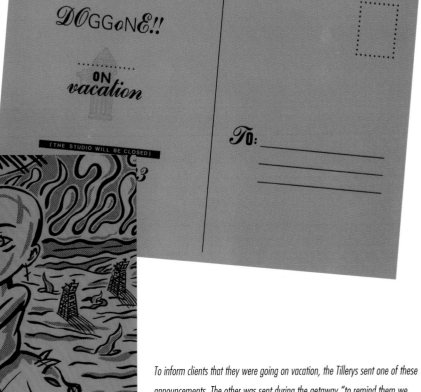

To inform clients that they were going on vacation, the Tillerys sent one of these announcements. The other was sent during the getaway "to remind them we were having a great time," says Val Tillery. "It was probably the weirdest, most surreal vacation announcement we'd ever seen done."

The theme of this tiny book entitled "Visitation"—that "it is worth the struggle" to be an artist—came to Val Tillery in the middle of the night. Appropriate for anyone in the industry, it was mailed to friends, supporters and clients of the studio for their encouragement. Hand-stamped in gold and printed in metallic ink, it was printed on the tail of another book-artist's press sheet and ran only $75 for an edition of six hundred.

To appeal to the local and regional design firms that account for their "bread and butter" work, the studio shunned the cold call and created these "mini-portfolios": handmade, gold-stamped, black boxes containing eight to ten laminated, offset-printed samples. The cost of each package was about six dollars.

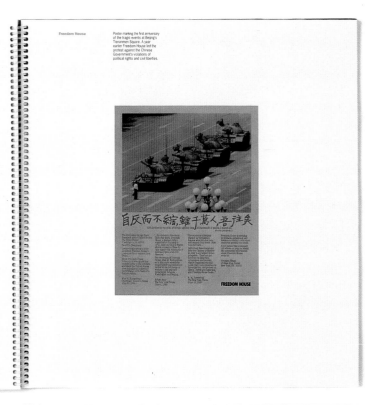

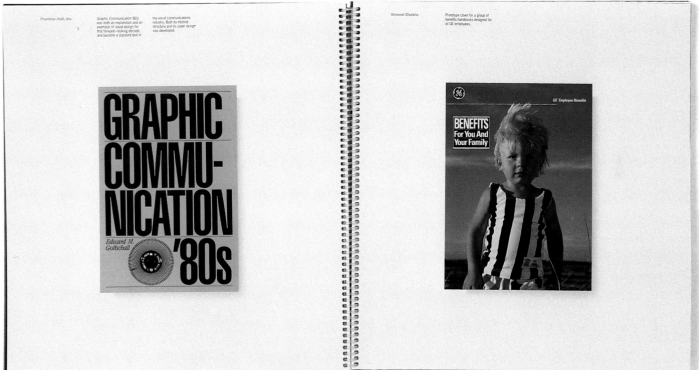

Simply and elegantly laid out on thick, coated paper, the pages of this limited-edition portfolio document the studio's unwavering commitment to the excellence and integrity of design. The 11 1/2" x 12",
eight-color, mechanically bound book is a paradigm of quality.

The first paragraph in the introduction to the limited edition portfolio of Emerson, Wajdowicz Studios, Inc. is earnest and succinct. It reads, simply, "The key to successful, powerful visual communications is quality." The following seventy-nine pages of this weighty book present an overview of the sophisticated and intelligent work done by the studio in the past ten years for some of the world's largest and most influential corporations, motion picture studios, and book and magazine publishers. Also included is the work the studio has done for cultural institutions and Freedom House, a human rights organization, for which the studio serves as design consultant. An expensive undertaking at over $100,000 for eight hundred books, the labor of love was delivered to current and former clients and friends in the United States and Europe.

Since its founding in 1967, White + Associates has been known as a corporate design firm. In the last few years, though, it has branched out into a greater variety of design areas, including point-of-purchase and packaging design, and entertaining and advertising. Illustrating its unique, artistic and conceptual talents is this timely and sincere 1990 holiday card. "We like to design a card every year," says art director Trina Carter Nuovo, "to give a personal touch to our client relations. As designers, it also allows us a bit more personal freedom to create than do the usual design projects." The theme of this particular card is "The Missing Peace," in which the important subjects of the time, such as the Gulf war, environmental problems and the recession are addressed. "But we did not want it to become too heavy or foreboding," explains Nuovo. "Thus, we combined it with the more holiday-type symbols of angels, arches, youth and hope." The hand-lettering lining the arch reads: "May the innocence of this joyous season continue through the year—that we might hold our fragile earth with wonder and humility." She adds, "it seemed to strike the right chord and definitely assured our clients that we were *aware*."

White + Associates 1990 holiday card sent to clients, fellow design firms, agencies, vendors, family and friends. The photography and paper were donated. Gilbert Paper's donation of the Esse stock was in appreciation of Ken White's part in designing the actual paper texture of the new Esse line. The two-color card was hand-cut and the envelopes were hand-folded by the staff.

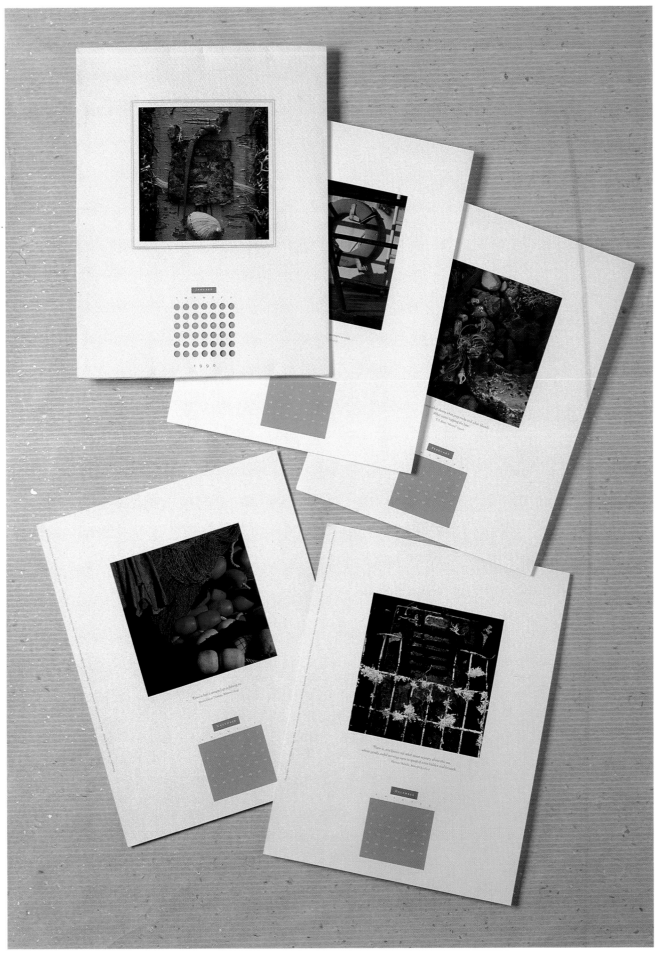

This 1990 calendar for Mercier/Wimberg, professional photographers, was intended to further attract corporate and advertising clients and bring in more creative projects as well. The theme is the sea, which gives ample opportunity for powerful imagery and interesting supporting quotes, and, says Trina Carter Nuovo, "includes images, colors and emotions that most people would feel comfortable enough with to hang it on their wall for the duration of a year."

Poster created for the North American Transplant Coordinators Organization, a group that acts as a forum for organ transplant coordinators from around the world. This "thank you" poster was intended to recognize those who have donated organs in the past. It positively portrays the system and suggests the emotional and human value in transplantation. It has also built awareness and resulted in more organ donors. Ten thousand posters were produced.

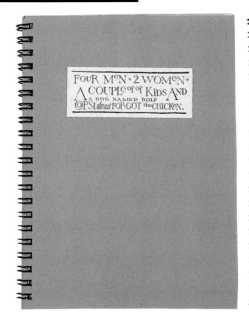

Annual report for the Triton Energy Corporation and subsequent 5 1/2" x 7 1/4" pick-up brochure for Unruh. The presentation, which shows some of Unruh's best illustration that year, drew three new clients, more annual report work and resulted in a $45,000 gain in income.

Instead of hiring an expensive, *National Geographic*-type photographer to visually convey their multinationality in their annual report, the Triton Energy Corporation went to illustrator Jack Unruh, who in turn received a savings from them. After forty thousand copies of the report were printed but still on the press, Unruh explains, "we took off the black line plate and ran about five hundred additional pages of each illustration." They were then trimmed down and spiral bound into an effective promotional brochure for himself. Although Unruh had drawn from photographs and scrap, the spontaneous and sketchy quality of the work make it seem that it was done by a straw-hatted Unruh on location. But, alas, like the man in James Taylor's song "Gorilla" (a part of which is quoted on the promotion's last page), he could only wish that he were there.

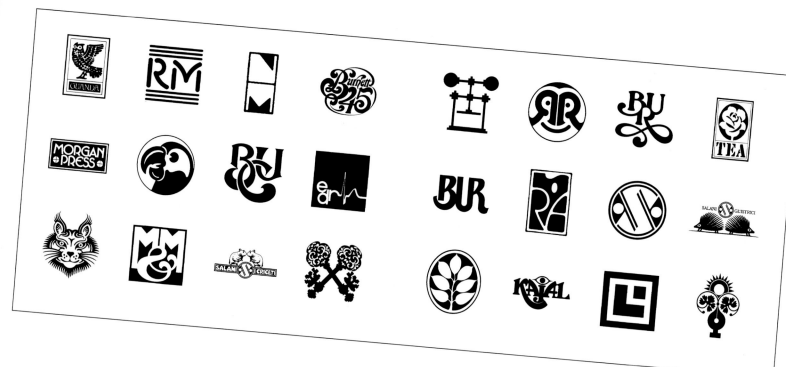

In the above folder, the late John Alcorn introduced to Americans his logo and colophon work, which has been long familiar to Europeans. "Many of these marks," he explained, "were created for Italy's leading publishing houses." Applied as the principal graphic element of covers and bindings, in promotional materials and advertising, the weighty and lush symbols project a clear and distinctive identity. The display typeface used on the cover was drawn by Alcorn in 1989 for his redesign of the Italian daily *Il Messaggero*. One thousand were mailed to publishing and corporate art directors and executives.

In the U.S., Alcorn was better known for his alternatively heavy graphic and lightly intricate illustration styles, both exemplified in these two paper promotions for Mohawk Paper Mills. Each is part of a distinct series, the design and illustration of which were inspired by the name of the particular paper being promoted.

LOGO & COLO-PHON

Printing of Alcorn's logo and colophon folder was donated by Morgan Press of Dobbs Ferry, New York, one of the companies whose logo Alcorn designed.

Two posters designed and illustrated by Alcorn for Mohawk Paper Mills. The style and image of each were inspired by the names of the papers featured.

The design, layout and type were computer generated. The separations of the numbered areas were output to film, while the face card areas were stripped in traditionally. By keeping as much as possible in the computer, the studio kept stripping and film costs low. The number of cards and their size were configured to work the sheet to its maximum usage.

Grafik seems to have something for everyone, a diversity of style that lends itself as well to sales brochures and posters as it does to annual reports and direct-mail promotions. Consistently clever and well suited to each client, their self-promotions, for example, project inventiveness and gaiety. Seeking a seasonal card that would serve to bring in new work, thank existing clients, and serve as a collectible, Grafik created this deck of cards in celebration of both the 1991 palindrome year and palindromes in general. Three thousand of the deck were produced at very little cost to the studio because virtually everything was donated. Each vendor involved contributed their very best and used the deck as a self-promotional tool for their own clients and vendors. It was an extremely successful promotion for all and garnered Grafik the Gilbert presentation box project (see page 25).

Grafik designed this presentation box for Gilbert Paper, which instructed the studio to provide a limited edition of the presentation kit to distribution specification representatives, showing traditional and nontraditional uses of their products. Grafik's concept is based on the idea that "beauty exists all around us in nature but is often overlooked."

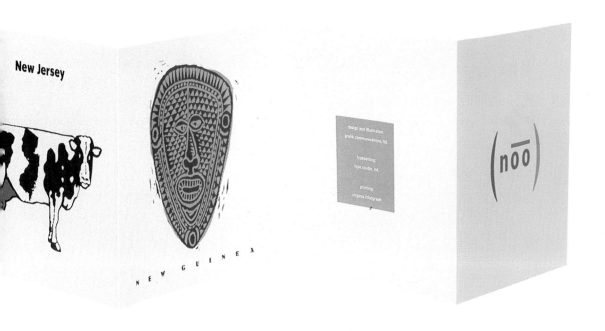

This six match color holiday card offered each member of the studio the opportunity to contribute their unique style and skill through the design of their own panel. The piece was offset printed via donation from Virginia Lithograph. The promotion resulted in many phone calls and stronger relations with existing clients.

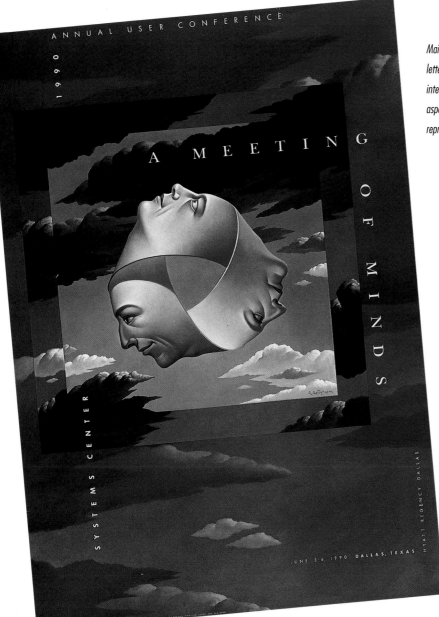

Mailed to users and managers of software, this two-part invitation (poster plus letterhead and brochure) announced an annual software user conference intended to share the latest information on products. To promote this "sharing" aspect of the conference, the firm searched for a cerebral illustration to represent "A Meeting of the Minds," and settled on the Mobius strip concept.

This pocket folder and final announcement are part of a five-piece series produced at a cost of $45,000 for the annual convention of the Sheet Metal and Air Conditioning Contractors' National Association. The vibrancy and strong graphics to the theme of "Unleash the Power" were well liked by the convention attendees.

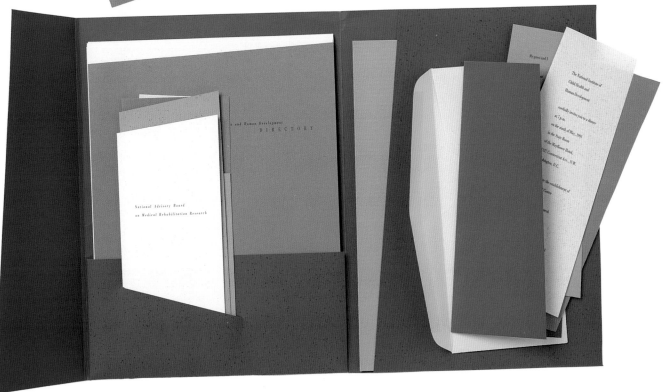

Designed for the National Center for Medical Rehabilitation Research, this simple but elegant package and dinner invitation present an array of texture, form and color. Twenty-five hundred of the folders and sets of conference materials and two hundred fifty dinner invitations were produced at a cost of $16,000. It drew another invitation project and various pocket folder projects for the studio.

Targeted toward the World Summit for Children in Washington, D.C. in 1990, this "Stick Up for Kids" poster, a freelance project of Melanie Bass, was produced to motivate children and their families to participate in the candlelight vigil campaign to fight world hunger. Not only did Bass devote her design expertise, but she also was responsible for calling up the various vendors for donations and coordinating their services. The kids loved it, and the stickers helped spread the word—on jackets, notebooks and lunch boxes.

Just because the majority of the world views a predominately solid background and 8 ¹/₂″ x 11″ size as the two essential characteristics of stationery, it doesn't mean that Rick Eiber does. In fact his primary objective in creating this set was "to create a new look for stationery to replace the globally recognized solution." While it is too soon to say whether he has achieved this lofty goal, he has done a commendable job of creating a unique letterhead, which successfully integrates his identity through the color of the studio's acronym and his self-portrait. Two thousand of the four-color sets were designed and offset printed at a cost of $2,500. The type and color separations were computer generated; the latter was done in trade. Eiber used density reduction to permit typing over the image.

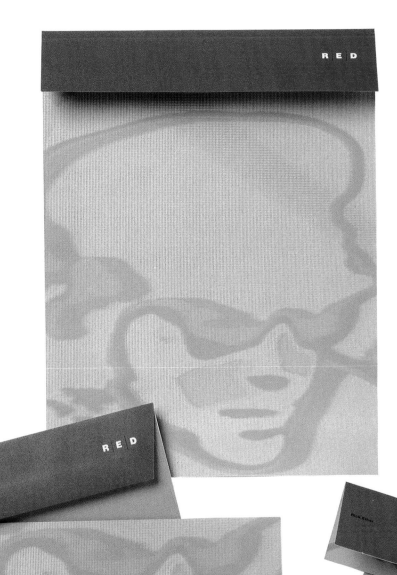

This stationery is representative of Eiber's design sensibility and originality and, says Eiber, "shows clients you can push limits to achieve uniqueness."

The firm saved money by using some of the magazine's separations and printing all of the copy separately before binding it in with the four color.

The objective of Michael Brock Design in creating a media kit for the visually lavish *L.A. Style* was to convey the uniqueness of this magazine and the attractive demographics of its readership— affluent, educated, young and single—"committed," as the publisher says, "to living well." A true expression of the magazine's identity, the kit is lovely to behold: elegant in design, regal in typography, striking in layout. As with the magazine itself, the large size of the kit creates ample space for the flow of the seductive and dreamy photography and graphics. Between five thousand and seventy-five hundred were produced at a cost of $40,000. The promotion has drawn six to twelve jobs for the firm.

This powerful black-and-white image is inspired by the American Indian and profoundly expresses what the demise of this culture suggests about the direction in which the human race is headed. The striking photograph, combined with the simple and elegant design and the high quality of its four-color reproduction, immediately impresses upon one the talent and expertise of the seven photographers of Greg Booth + Associates. Fifteen hundred of the posters were sent to international and national designers, art directors and creative directors, and in all likelihood ended up on a great many office walls. In fact, the studio has received over three hundred complimentary phone calls to date, many of which have materialized into projects for the studio. The production of the piece ran an estimated $4,000, about 25 percent of the studio's annual self-promotional budget.

The design, layout, type and color separations of "Canyon de Chelly" were computer-generated, output to Linotronic. It was offset printed in four color.

LINDA SCHARF / ILLUSTRATION
240 HEATH STREET SUITE 311
BOSTON, MA 02130-1199

Some clients:
ACP Observer
Bank of Boston
Boston Globe
Bull HN Information Systems
CMP Publications
Delaware Today
East/West Journal
Fidelity Investments
Genzyme
G.K. Hall Books
L.A. Times
Lotus
New Age Magazine
Personnel Journal
Seventeen
Stereo Review
Walking Magazine
Whittle Communications

Art photographed by Clements/Howcroft

To bring her work to the attention of those who might commission illustration in a similar vein from her, Scharf mails her new work out in one- to four-color postcard format throughout the year. The backside of each lists some of her clients, which range from the Boston Globe and the Los Angeles Times to Houghton Mifflin and G.K. Hall Books.

Dance movement is conveyed in visual terms for the Goucher College Dance/ Movement Therapy Master's degree program catalog cover. As well, the image is used on an accompanying poster to further attract interest from potential students.

Pro bono project for Global ReLeaf, an environmental project through which concerned citizens can learn how to improve the environment. The file folder contains a curriculum guide. This, along with a poster of the same image, was mailed to elementary school teachers nationwide.

"So much of promotion seems to be luck and chance and intuition," says the talented hand-letterer and illustrator Linda Scharf, adding that it is difficult to quantify the "success" of her or her clients' promotional pieces. The point of her postcard promotions is simply to present her new work to current and prospective advertising, editorial and publishing clients and let the work speak for itself. For each print run of three thousand, the cost is usually $500. The power of her illustration, she says, may be that it is able "to reach people on a level where words don't."

The Goucher College catalog and the Global ReLeaf folder covers convey the degree to which this is true. Scharf's work, through color, texture, image and close contact with other creatives, presents the spirit of her clients' needs. "Most of the projects I work on," she says, "seem to be very organic and layered—an interactive process among client, designer, copywriter and illustrator."

To generate employee response, Schering-Plough commissioned Scharf to illustrate an employee referral brochure, poster, bookmark and pin. Twelve thousand brochures and two hundred posters were produced. The copywriter followed Scharf's visual lead; about referral he writes, "It's a Fine Art."

It was not happenstance that Gina Federico's wedding date lent itself so favorably to the design of her announcement. "I made sure we got married on a date," she explains, "that I could have fun with." The inventive piece, which had a production cost of $300, shows that "you can do something as serious and cloaked in tradition as get married and still have a playful sense of humor about it."

Humor also played a part in the invitation she created for the Type Director Club's annual award ceremony, honoring an individual who has made a major contribution in the field of typography. Federico happens to have an intimate knowledge of the man as well as his work, three pieces of which are featured in the collage that spells his name. Gene, she says, "is a great designer, who I happen to call Daddy!"

Federico's one-color, offset-printed wedding announcement brought an enthusiastic response on the part of the three hundred fifty family members, friends and acquaintances it was sent to. Thus, there were many wonderful gifts and "a great party."

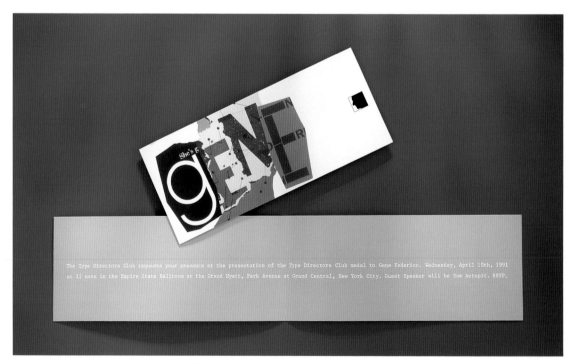

Bargaining the printer down to as low a price as possible, Federico was able to use the money she saved for a fifth color and varnish. Fifteen hundred were produced at a cost of $1,570, excluding the design, which Federico donated.

I & Company's two-color accordion announcement and letterhead proves appropriate for a range of existing and prospective clients, from corporate to the more unconventional. It is run off the studio's LaserWriter II printer as needed.

When Carol B. Neiley decided to open her own design studio, she chose a name that she would grow into. The consequent visual identity program she developed was the result of the "I" neatly playing off "eye," and is intended to represent her unique visual communication. When the studio opened in 1991, Neiley created the above accordion mailer to say, with a blink, "We're open for business." One thousand were produced at a cost of $500 and mailed to existing clients, suppliers and friends at a rate of fifty a month. "Almost everyone I called remembered it," she says, "so I got in the door and was able to set up appointments." Consequently, she landed five new jobs and received an estimated $15,000 in revenue.

Each year Pinkhaus designs their Christmas party invitation and greeting with a particular theme. In 1990 it was "recycling," a subject conveyed in method as well as message: A logo designed by staff designer Claudia De Castro to promote a Christmas tree recycling program in Florida was then recycled onto Pinkhaus' Christmas invitation and decorative building banners. The pieces work on a personal as well as a "universal" level, for the recipients are reminded of the party and drivers-by are encouraged to recycle their trees.

With regard to client promotions, the firm deftly devises strong concept and imagery and utilizes production technique that appropriately illustrates each client's unique capabilities. To announce the new logo and new location of one of southern Florida's oldest printing firms, for example, Pinkhaus designed a distinctive and amusing brochure in three match colors, black and varnish. Its "portraits" communicate that Rex Three is "a designer's best friend" and that "the old dog has learned new tricks."

▼ *Christmas party invitation that in addition to announcing the gala affair, explains the local recycling program and its advantage. Part of the copy reads, "By taking your tree to a collection center instead of throwing it out in the trash, you'll be giving it a second life as mulch in our local parks."*

▲ *Located on a busy street, the firm's building gets a lot of exposure. The two silk-screened banners, which complement the firm's Christmas party invitation and greeting, cost approximately $1,000 to produce. The colors were designed to be common on both sides, and images were kept down so that only two screens were needed.*

▶ *Inspired by the client's name Rex Three, Inc. and the fact that this old-time printer was moving into a larger, newer facility, Pinkhaus used color, size, and striking photography of man's best friend to make the 7 3/4" x 14" brochure highly amusing and memorable. The piece shows off the printing, engraving and separation capabilities of the client. Five thousand were produced. It was completely different from anything they had ever mailed out to prospects, and it caught people's attention.*

THEY SAY YOU CAN'T TEACH
AN OLD DOG NEW TRICKS.
BUT, AS WITH EVERY RULE,
THERE ARE EXCEPTIONS.
SIT, REX. DANCE, REX.
SING, REX. MAKE MY ANNUAL
REPORT LOOK SENSATIONAL, REX.

woof!

REX 2

To set the image of WJMK, a television production company in Boca Raton, as exciting and progressive, Pinkhaus utilized artful imagery, handsome typography and high-quality printing to convey the company's distinctive personality. Five thousand were printed in five color.

COUCOU!

Promotion for photographer Nick Norwood. The poster-size piece emphasizes the sensuality of his work and the degree to which his black-and-white images communicate the universality of body language.

CZY WOLNO FOTOGRAFOWAĆ?

JAG

HAR

BRATTOM

The sprightly illustration of R.O. Blechman is readily identifiable. It is spare, jiggly and thoughtfully positioned against a roomy backdrop of space. As founder of The Ink Tank, an illustration and state-of-the-art animation studio, Blechman has drawn a great many clients and talented artists as a result of his unconventionality and sophistication. The studio's promotions take a soft-sell approach; hence, the name of their newspaper, *Soft Cel,* an "occasional publication." Replete with interviews, announcements, sports and, of course, a funnies page, the timely, informational and visual format allows the animators to freely and humorously point out their capabilities.

Equally clever is the Christmas card on the facing page, inspired by Russian stack dolls. It in turn inspired the idea for their 1992 Christmas card. "We received a complaint," Blechman says, "that the amount of paper used was unecological." Thus, the Ink Tank's next greeting will be made out of recycled cards from past years.

Initially sent out as a mailer to promote the services of their animation studio, the four-page, offset-printed newspaper now accompanies the Ink Tank's sample animation reel. Three thousand papers were produced at a little more than one dollar per copy. The artists donated their work.

The donated illustrations of Mark Marek, Steven Guarnaccia, Gary Baseman and Ron Barrett all fit into one another, with an illustration by R.O. Blechman and a balloon with the logo designed by Seymour Chwast at its center.

Blechman opted for this original stand-up, die-cut, desk card format over the posters Adweek had originally requested. This four-color piece was done in trade with the magazine, granting the studio advertising space in return.

R.O. Blechman illustrated and Louise Fili designed this pro bono invitation for the Music Theatre Group. Inspired by Hamlet, at a cost of about forty cents per copy, it presents an alternative, says Blechman, to the "deadly dull and humorless" tone of a typical fundraising solicitation.

It can't be very often that an art director receives a promotional piece that she can *do* as well as look at. Enter Robert de Michiell's version of a children's activity book. Five hundred of these saddle-stitched books were produced for $900, about 20 percent of de Michiell's annual self-promotion budget. Sent to clients and art directors, the book presents de Michiell's ability to come up with original and amusing concepts and render them in dynamic style.

The same can be said for his thematic mailers, evocative of the emotions we experience as a result of each season. "Summertime Blues," de Michiell says was the one that most struck a chord with people. Fifteen hundred of each were produced at a cost of $2,100.

"Book O' Fun," an interactive piece, is de Michiell's version of a children's activity book. The fun and stylized book was copied, collated and stapled at a copy shop.

To save money, de Michiell used the same mechanical on each card, only changing the image. The four-color promotions were scanned on laser and offset printed.

Combining intense color, bold typography and arresting design, the work of Michael Mabry Design often presents a fresh language for the age-old messages of retail identity, packaging, advertising and corporate communications. To announce and draw attention to an AIGA New York presentation on color, for example, Mabry looked at the scientific aspects of color, rather than the subjective properties each of the speakers would address.

Standing out in the deluge of paper promotions each year is Mabry's series for Strathmore, showcasing the printability and overall look of the papers. The three books are impressive—unique individually and consistent as a series. "Esprit" addressed printing techniques, "Rhododendron" revolved around the relationship of stress to work, and "Americana" looked at the historical imagery from design's past. At a cost of approximately $1.30 per copy, the promotion functions both as a sample and as interesting reading material and imagery. They certainly spurred new interest in both the papers and the studio. After the second promotion was sent out, Strathmore saw sales increase by 20 percent, while Mabry estimates the studio received ten to fifteen calls per book.

Seventy thousand copies of "Esprit," eighty thousand copies of "Rhododendron," and eighty-five thousand copies of "Americana" were sent to graphic designers, printers and paper distributors. A wide variety of printing and bindery techniques were used to showcase the papers.

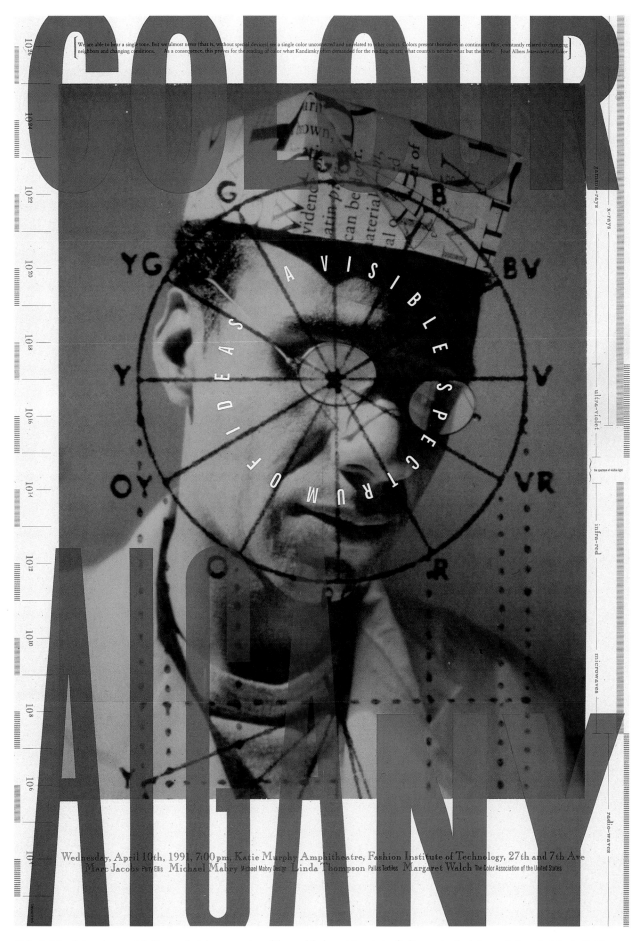

Mabry took the photograph, generated all type on the in-house computer and then used the laser printer output as final typography. The design, production and printing had to take place in one and one-half weeks, so Mabry was unable to refine the design or correct the color on the pass. The design was donated.

In this metaphorical series for James H. Barry Printing, its capabilities and level of quality in lithography are compared to other well-designed products. The series was designed in trade.

Five hundred calendars were allotted for fundraisers for the Art Directors Club of New York, New Jersey and Philadelphia, which also staged exhibitions of the original work. Each of the four illustrators received two hundred copies to distribute as a soft-sell promotion and as an addition to each of their own individual advertising campaigns.

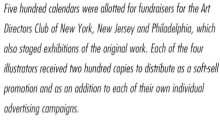

The idea for "The Daily Palette," a first-of-its-kind calendar developed specifically for the graphic arts community, was born among illustrator friends Andrea Mistretta, Jack Moore, Federico Castelluccio and Rich Grote, and by their mutual desire to do a collaborative project. "The idea was," explains Mistretta, "to provide us with the opportunity to create new illustration with somewhat more personal freedom than we'd experience on an 'actual job,' then accompany the art with an information-filled planning calendar which would provide us with year-long exposure to our general target market." The collaboration became larger when the four illustrators received the backing of designer Nina Ovryn; Mohawk Paper Mills, which provided $27,000, including the premium matte-coated paper; and the six-color printer, Waldman Graphics, which covered the rest. Mistretta and Moore diligently gathered a wealth of information—birthdates of influential designers, design studios, publications and art-related products; contest deadlines; and quotes to provoke and inspire. The sidebar of each calendar page presents "Call for Entries" information.

Yvonne Buchanan creates a calendar to promote her work every year, a form ideal for this illustrator because it grants her the chance to exhibit her work in a series—to share her art and her social and political consciousness. Ideally, it stays up all year. Goaded by her overwhelming sense of the "woes of the world," her 1991 calendar offers images of everything from the savings and loan debacle to racism and the oppression of women to the problems of AIDS and the homeless to urban pollution and crime. Over $3,000 of her annual self-promotion budget went into this two-color, offset printed project. A mailing of five hundred to magazine and advertising art directors and art buyers resulted in $21,500 in revenue, largely due to one particular ad account. As well, "several newspapers such as the *Washington Post* rediscovered me," she says. "Also I've become involved with a group of political cartoonists who do visual commentary on current events—which I'm extremely happy about."

This calendar shows Buchanan's work and her way of thinking—all year 'round. About 60 percent of its recipients called to offer Buchanan a job or project.

Chamlee created one hundred of this sixteen-page, thread-sewn book at the low cost of $250. The main story was computer designed, output to Linotronic, and lead Linotype was used for the other type; the dates were set by hand in wood. It was letterpressed on paper donated by Castle Press.

Following two marriages and two divorces, Rebecca Chamlee underwent a bit of an identity crisis, which culminated one day in 1991 when, she writes in this small booklet sent to one hundred clients, friends and family members, "My pen poised above the check, for a second I couldn't remember my name." Once Chamlee came to and realized she was backed by Amy Vanderbilt, she declared, "The Name Remains the Same," and created this booklet to say it was so. Employing four colors and four typefaces to convey the dates, the turning points of her life's story, the presence and then disappearance of her middle and last names, and various excerpts from etiquette books, she says, "I wanted to do a wholly typographic piece to remind me of why I fell in love with design in the first place."

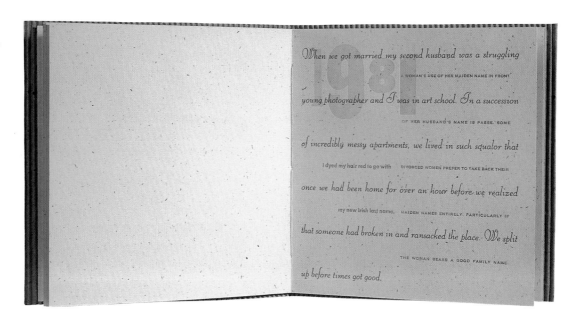

"A boomerang always comes back, just as I want my clients to come back," says Sheri Seibold of her graphic design firm's namesake. The boomerang motif figures prominently in her self-promotions, for which she sets aside $800 annually. Five hundred dollars of it was spent on three hundred sets of sample folders, stationery and business cards, packages which were sent to potential clients and other design studios "to portray," she says, "the lighthearted, whimsical, almost humorous character" of her design. Although she saved money on hand-cutting the interior's wavy edges, she says she'd pay for it next time.

On the other hand, with The Deckled Edge, her handmade card and paper company, she expects most of the work to require her hand, for each piece she creates is evocative of days gone by, a time when cards were not mass produced, but created one at a time with tenderness. Yet they also are in sync with the ecological sensibility of our times and appeal to many of her design clients for this reason.

This activity guide for a family reunion of Maranatha Volunteers International exemplifies the meeting ground for Boomerang Design and The Deckled Edge. "It fits," says Seibold, "the client's request for a homey, familial feel, and the organic shapes and natural paper fits the convention setting of Yosemite National Park." Seven hundred of the two-color pieces were designed, typeset and offset printed at a cost of $1,100.

Boomerang design package, mailed to potential clients, other design studios — anyone who requests samples of the studio's work. The stationery, cards and envelopes were offset printed, while the folder was screen printed.

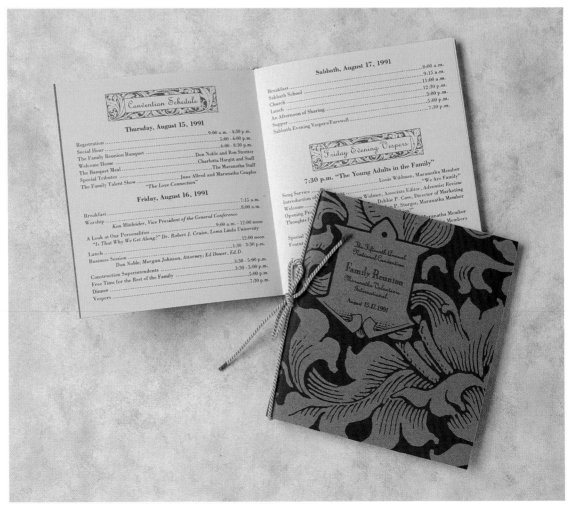

With her stationary, Siebold simply and elegantly displays the hand-crafted, -painted and -assembled pieces she desires to sell, while her unusual business card "reveals the special sensations that handmade paper provides." The time consuming, inexpensively produced set (one dollar each) has resulted in three to four new projects thus far.

For Earth Day, Seibold created twenty of these promotions at a cost of $20, using handmade paper, a creative binding technique (a tree twig), and the occasion itself (when "people are thinking about natural materials and processes"). The piece was photocopied and hand-painted.

Sent to friends, relatives and "clients who would appreciate it," this handsome, nostalgic valentine conveys Seibold's commitment to small details and personal craftsmanship. The design, layout and type were done on the computer, and the laser-printed pieces were hand-painted. Forty-five were produced at a cost of $25.

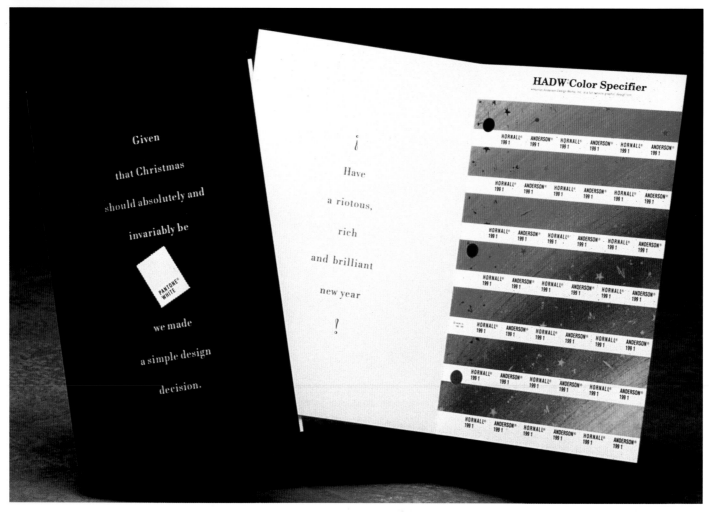

The layout and type of this six-color pun on Pantone was computer generated and offset printed in trade with Print Northwest. The hot stamp was also donated.

The challenge that Hornall Anderson Design Works sets for itself with each new promotion is to create a piece that stands out among all the others — whether it be a holiday card, packaging or a calendar. Sights are set on defying standards, both cerebrally and visually, and, if possible, having fun in the process. The above New Year's card, for example, presents a pun on Pantone and color chips.

Sometimes, as with the holiday gift on the facing page, the studio tries for both versatility and client participation. There were four possible ways to distribute this piece: a poster; a die-cut poster, which the individual could punch, fold and make ornaments from; twelve single ornaments sent anonymously until the final mailing—the poster—identified the sender; or pre-assembled ornaments in a box.

This six-color poster was printed in trade with Print Northwest. The piece greeted and thanked clients, prospects, family and friends in both two- and three-dimensional format.

In printing this packaging for Italia, an Italian restaurant, deli, bakery, caterer, wine shop and art gallery, a split fountain was used for maximum effect at a lower cost.

One of the strengths of the Italia campaign is that elements from the symbol can be extracted and featured individually or together. Design time was traded for Italia's food and beverages.

Announcement and invitation for the integration of two architectural firms and its new name, Integrus Architecture. Using mostly recyclable materials, it portrays Integrus' sensitivity to the environment.

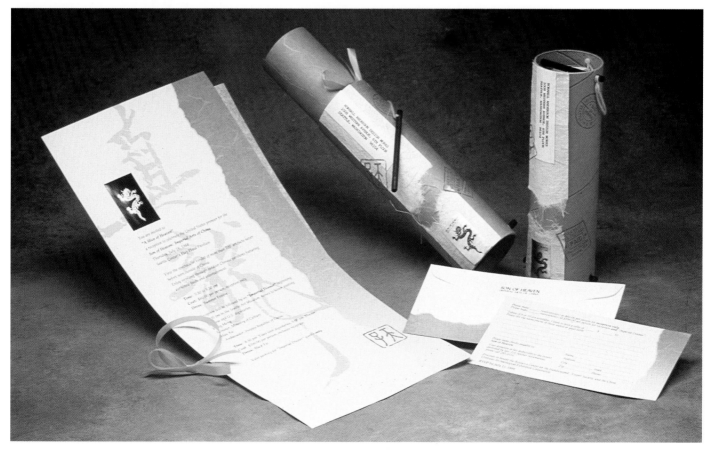

This direct-mail invitation to the opening gala celebration of "Son of Heaven," a limited, special tour of imperial art from ancient China, was hot-stamped, embossed, pad-stamped and hand-assembled. It both captured the mood and sold out the event.

One of the ten annual promotions done for photographer Jim Laser. Each positions the man as a world-class photographer, beautifully displays his work, and serves as an attractive and useful gift and catalog. This one focuses on his recent travels to Japan.

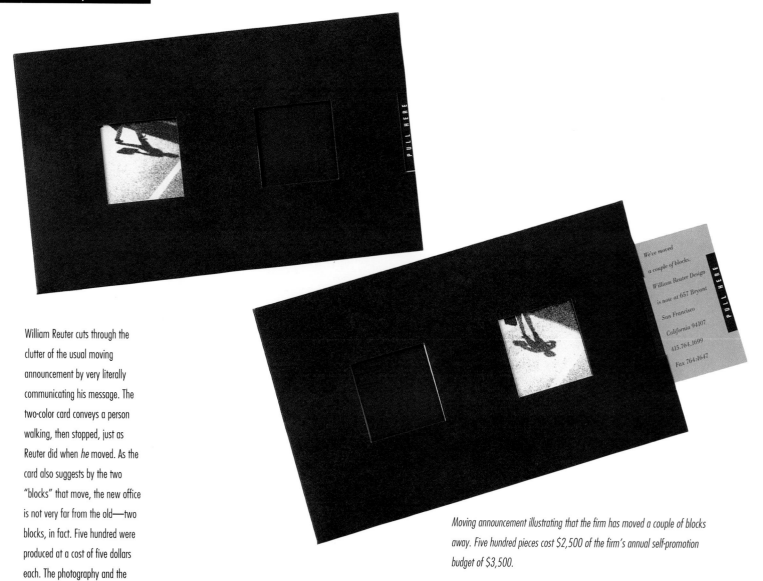

William Reuter cuts through the clutter of the usual moving announcement by very literally communicating his message. The two-color card conveys a person walking, then stopped, just as Reuter did when *he* moved. As the card also suggests by the two "blocks" that move, the new office is not very far from the old—two blocks, in fact. Five hundred were produced at a cost of five dollars each. The photography and the assembly were done in-house. It was mailed to clients, suppliers and friends. The announcement resulted in about fifty phone calls for Reuter and ten to twenty new jobs, including promotional pieces, folders and brochures.

Moving announcement illustrating that the firm has moved a couple of blocks away. Five hundred pieces cost $2,500 of the firm's annual self-promotion budget of $3,500.

The design and illustration of Michael Schwab is bold and dramatic, and it simply and quickly gets to the point. While it is often difficult to determine when and how a concept originates, Schwab is able to pinpoint the inspirations for these two promotions, both of which arose from film. His 1991 moving announcement was inspired by a scene from the recent film *Green Card*, while it was old black-and-white footage of the 1936 Olympic Games that inspired the design of his "Join Up" poster. Both were inexpensive to produce. Three hundred copies of the moving announcement cost $200; the type, which was designed for another project, is all hand-lettered. It was printed on a letterpress and was mailed to existing and potential advertising and design clients.

"Join Up" was created for the Oklahoma State University Rowing Club at a cost of $200 for fifty one-color screen prints. It is the accurate and direct depiction of concept that makes the piece work. Explains Schwab, "The sport of rowing is powerful—no frills—and so are the athletes."

Michael Schwab's card announcing his move from San Francisco to Sausalito. The bold design was printed on a letterpress. Three hundred were produced for $200.

MICHAEL SCHWAB DESIGN

IS MOVING TO

80 LIBERTY SHIP WAY N°7

SAUSALITO, CA 94965 415 331-7621

Poster commissioned by the Oklahoma State University Rowing Club to get other athletes to "join up" and become members. Fifty of the compelling posters were positioned around the OSU campus.

Gunn Associates' current self-promotional brochure is so thoroughly comprehensive that it starts from the beginning, meaning the very beginning of design history for each of the firm's six areas of expertise: corporate identity, annual reports, packaging, promotional materials, industrial design and illustration. Each of the elegantly written introductions smoothly leads into impressive examples, beautifully reproduced, of the firm's expertise. The high-quality of the book, president David Lizotte says, shows that "we care about our business enough to invest a substantial marketing effort, so clients can be assured that we can do a good job for them also." Substantial it was, at about nine dollars per book.

The brochure on the facing page was done for Boston Corporate Art and gives the art consultancy a high-quality and professional image. Not only does it show actual examples of projects the consultancy has completed, says Lizotte, but it also stimulates potential clients to review their own environment.

The color separations for this four-color brochure were computer generated, output to Linotronic. It has yielded well over two hundred phone calls, four hundred jobs and resulted in an increase in the sorts of packaging jobs the studio had desired.

Ten thousand of this brochure were produced for $38,000, of which $18,000 went into location photography. It was
mailed to major corporations in the Boston area. Five match colors were used on the cover, four process colors in the text.

It seems people have always had something to say about Kay Williams Graphics Consulting. "Y'all's name's too long," our clients in West Texas said. "Wow dudes, that name is like radically lengthy," our California accounts told us. "Jah mon, dis name wa-a-ay too beeg," commented our Caribbean clients. On every Florida business trip we heard, "¡Oye! ¡Su nombre es muy largo!" Even New York cabbies told us, "Yo! Kay! Dat name is <u>so</u> <u>freakin'</u> long!" So finally, we decided to move on changing it.

Kay Williams Graphics Consulting has moved to a shorter name (KWGC) and a taller location (2911 Turtle Creek Blvd., Suite 650, Dallas, Texas 75219). Call us at the same number (214-987-4377) or fax us (214-528-2862) for creative marketing communication that's very long on results.

This moving and name change announcement was sent to clients, vendors and friends during a three-week period—before and during the move. It brought a great many phone calls and chuckles.

When Kay Williams Graphic Consulting moved to a taller location (a sixth floor), she decided to make her name shorter at the same time. "Everyone always commented on how long our name was," she says, "so we decided to make a joke out of it." To let their clients in on the changes, they produced five hundred of these humorous, five-color 8 1/2" x 4" cards at under $2,500.

Humor and innovation figure into KWGC's holiday and client promotions as well. Neither their 1989 nor their 1990 holiday greetings are cards per se. Instead, one is a plastic-coated banner accompanied by bars of chocolate. While the chocolate was quick to disappear, the banner stuck around and was used over and over again by the clients and vendors who received it. It won many awards, says Williams, and drew one new client. Equally atypical and reusable was the following year's seasonal promotion in which the agency's corporate colors were lit up for all to see.

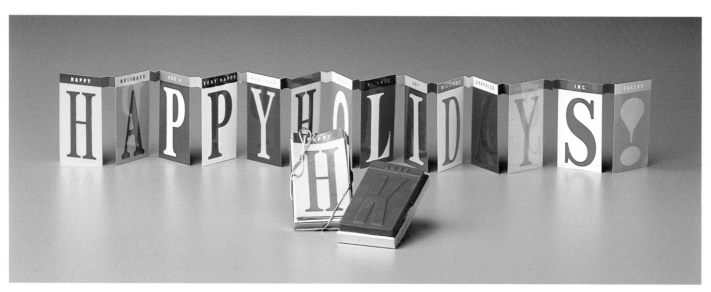

Offset printed and then plastic coated on both sides, all were folded by the agency, which Kay Williams now thinks was a time-consuming mistake. Yet production costs were under $5,000 for five hundred.

Two hundred of the KWGC "Light Up" promotions were produced at under $5,000. The five-color card and Plexiglas candle holder set were hand-delivered and mailed during the holiday season.

Shon Wood's name is an appropriate one for a paper specification rep. To announce the birth of her baby, KWGC donated their design services and ingeniously tied together "Wood," paper and baby by using tree rings to symbolize the maturation of the family—from the birth of Wood and her husband to the birth of their child.

Teaser for Butler paper's new corporate color...you guessed it. One of the five witty and fun postcards was sent out every two weeks. Yet there are more to come: "It's a series," Williams says, "so it can be continued endlessly." The four-color pieces were hand-tinted with markers.

As Ellen Shapiro has discovered over the years, there are similarities between the designer/client relationship and the therapist/patient one. Before being able to help the client with its identity, the designer must first determine what the client wants. The ensuing confusion can sometimes cause the designer to throw up her hands and in exasperation exclaim a similar question (bar one word) to Freud's "What do women really want?" Shapiro has recently written a book on the subject entitled *Clients and Designers*, for which she interviewed clients all over the country in the quest of discovering what they're really looking for. To encourage people to come and hear about it at the Art Directors Club of New York, Shapiro designed and Victor Juhász illustrated this flyer that caused the recipients to first laugh and then talk about the issues that are important to them and their industry. "It worked," Shapiro says, for it was "easy and quick, cost next to nothing" ($300 for the production of two thousand), and resulted in a "standing room only crowd."

The Art Directors Club presents Ellen Shapiro on

What do clients really want?

THE SAFEST, MOST BORING ROUTE

TO CHANGE THEIR MINDS A MILLION TIMES

ANNOYING AS CRAZY EDDIE

THIS COULDN'T BE TRUE, SHE'S HAVING PARANOID DELUSIONS

EVERYTHING FOR NOTHING

TO HAGGLE OVER SILLY DETAILS

WORK ON SPEC

SOMETHING AS

AS RING AROUND THE COLLAR

TO DRIVE ME INSANE

SOMETHING AS CREATIVE

Why are creative types and clients so often at odds? Graphic designer Ellen Shapiro will try to cut through the smokescreen. Author of the critically acclaimed book, *Clients and Designers*, she has interviewed clients all across the country to analyze what they're really looking for— and it's not so depressing after all. Find out for yourself on Wednesday, April 10th at 12:30 pm at the Art Directors Club.

The Art Directors Club, Inc.
250 Park Avenue South (near 20th Street)
New York, NY 10003

Please call the Club for lunch reservations
(212) 674-0500

Illustration: Victor Juhász

Flyer announcing talk by Ellen Shapiro at the New York Art Directors Club. The piece demanded little in the way of time or money: The design, layout and type were computer generated, output to Linotronic; it was offset printed by a mailing house; the illustration was donated; and the copy ideas were suggested by Joan Dim, a longtime friend and client of Shapiro's.

Christopher Madison, president of ColorGraphics, a Los Angeles-based lithographer, went to his long-time design firm Rusty Kay & Associates with his idea for his company's holiday gift. He thought a tree would be unique and show ColorGraphics' concern for the environment, but, he said, he didn't want the tone to be preachy or opportunistic. The result is this pine-scented "deluxe air freshener," described as the "most effective on the market," containing the "active ingredient Chorophyll Maximus II." It was accompanied by planting instructions and a brief note from Madison. It was mailed to three thousand customers and suppliers in Los Angeles, San Francisco and Hawaii. The tree also served as an environmental inspiration to ColorGraphics employees with an altered message from Madison. The president is clearly pleased with the results: "It's the best thing we've ever done," he says. "I've had more letters and comments from customers who have responded to this promotion than to any other."

Pine seedling in 2 ¹/₂" x 14" box designed in trade for the lithographer ColorGraphics. Three thousand in all went out to customers and employees. The 1950s look is an outgrowth of the air freshener idea and nostalgic postwar advertising design. The serious yet humorous copy by Dave Chapple drove the design. Part of it reads: "If every American family utilized just one, over one billion pounds of smelly greenhouse gases would be removed from the atmosphere every year."

When Marianne Mitten, former senior designer and project manager for Morla Design, ventured out on her own, she needed a particular type of letterhead and announcement to come with her. They had to be of high quality, but not too expensive; make her look established and credible; convey her approach toward design (including the business and process); and be unusual enough to be remembered. Mitten thus created pieces that are unique in their own right and yet, through type treatment and color, tie in nicely together. To some extent, it just sort of happened that way. "I did three business card designs," says Mitten, "because I couldn't make up my mind which I liked best."

The strength of Mitten's announcement lies in its offbeat characteristics—in its size, shape, color and dangling business card—as well as its balance of the practical with the aesthetic. In case she moved, Mitten says, "I could print a new business card and still use the announcement. The four sheets behind the announcement were quick printed and inexpensive, so I can always alter the information, update it quickly and reprint it for under one hundred dollars." Two thousand announcements were produced at a cost of $1.50 each.

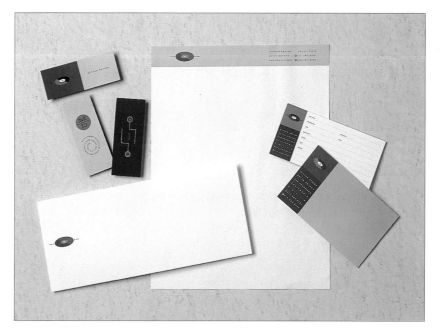

The total cost for 2,500 letterhead, 1,000 envelopes, 2,500 mailing labels, and 1,000 of each of the business cards ran to $3,200. Mitten is satisfied with all but the "sickly beige" color on the letterhead, business card and mailing label. This was a result of screening back the green color, she says.

Mitten says she learned a couple of things in hindsight: that the piece would have fit more comfortably into a file cabinet if it had been three-quarters of an inch shorter and perhaps would have been more effective if she'd added additional pages with four-color samples of her work. As it stands though, the thirteen-color piece has been a success, drawing six new clients.

"When you see a good design," says Keith Bright in his introduction to the firm's capabilities brochure, "you can feel it in your gut." Through bold photographs, attractive type and dynamic layout, this large-scale, perfect-bound book conveys to prospective clients just what Bright means by "good design" and how thorough research and thoughtful analysis are an integral part of the definition.

"A tour through space without words" is how designer Janice Okamura describes the beautiful, small booklet to the right created in celebration of 901 Washington Boulevard in Venice, California, the firm's new offices. Because every attempt was made to design the new facilities to retain the spirit and style of the former owners, designers Charles and Ray Eames, the design of this book was intended to convey via "art-book" quality the integrity and loveliness of the space.

Five thousand of the six-color, offset-printed books were produced at a cost of $120,000. They are periodically updated to include recent work.

The entire interior needed to fit on one press so the computer-generated design, layout and type were planned accordingly. The printing services were donated by Anderson Printing; the six-color separations were donated by Heinz Weber, Inc.; and $30,000 of an annual self-promotion budget of $50,000 was spent on the project.

All services were donated to the Childrens Institute for Eye Research in creating this powerful expression of the nonprofit organization's dedication to the eradication of childhood blindness. The sensitive photography, softness of typefaces and paper, and the treatment of the organization's symbol on the front cover all add up to impact. They successfully reinforce and help project the organization's image, legitimacy and professionalism.

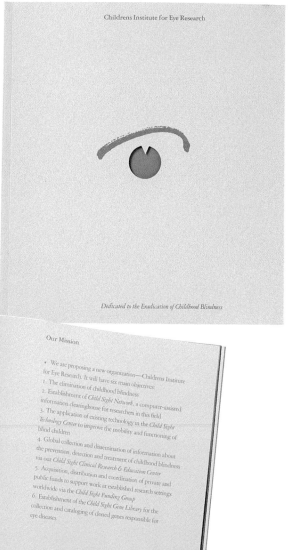

Our Mission

* We are proposing a new organization—Childrens Institute for Eye Research. It will have six main objectives:
1. The elimination of childhood blindness
2. Establishment of *Child Sight Network*, a computer-assisted information clearinghouse for researchers in this field
3. The application of existing technology in the *Child Sight Technology Center* to improve the mobility and functioning of blind children
4. Global collection and dissemination of information about the prevention, detection and treatment of childhood blindness via our *Child Sight Clinical Research & Education Center*
5. Acquisition, distribution and coordination of private and public funds to support work at established research settings worldwide via the *Child Sight Funding Group*
6. Establishment of the *Child Sight Gene Library* for the collection and cataloging of cloned genes responsible for eye diseases

Organization

* The Los Angeles-based Administrative Center will be the organization's focal point. It will house a small, skilled staff of planners, fund raisers, information technology specialists, publishers, conference organizers, and administrators. It will be managed by a Board-selected President.
* Research will be performed by leaders in related disciplines affiliated with any innovative hospital, research center or university, worldwide. Participants will have access to the Institute's funding and resources like Child Sight Network, our regular publications, videotapes, seminars and the Clinical Research & Education Center.
* Our Board of Directors will include the project's founders, major donors and leaders drawn from the business and scientific communities.
* The Board of Scientific Advisors will include participants invited from the World Health Organization, the Association of Pediatric Ophthalmology and Strabismus, and major university departments of ophthalmology.

Lisa Freeman's conviction that "before anyone can commit to environmental action, they must decide—in their own minds—why the planet is worth saving" was the fuel that fired her thoughtful 1990 brochure. In this "Earth Book," she presents the varied responses from the illustrators she represents, thus creating an excellent showcase for the unique conceptual and stylistic talents of each, as well as a provocative keepsake for its recipients. The piece was sent to designers and advertising, editorial and corporate art directors. It proved a very appropriate tie-in to the twentieth anniversary of Earth Day.

The six-color "Earth Book" was printed on a speckletone, recycled stock. Four thousand were produced at a cost of $2,000. The printing, typesetting and separations were donated.

The studio's capabilities brochure, intended to bring in both capabilities brochure and annual report work. The piece succeeds in showcasing past projects, as well as presenting a tangible representation of their annual report work.

With River City Studio's promotions, the medium is much of the message. The above capabilities brochure, for example, was created in the form of an annual report to bring in these two types of corporate design projects—annual reports and capabilities brochures. Designer Debra Turpin says the message it presents is that "River City Studio is a design firm that treats marketing and communications as a business." Five hundred sixty-five were produced for $15,000, and it has, estimates Turpin, brought in ten times that amount in revenue.

In a similar vein, promotional t-shirts were created to appeal to retail clothing manufacturers, small clothing stores, and other retail clothing and card and poster manufacturers to get clothing and/or point-of-purchase graphic jobs. Silk-screened t-shirts were presented in balsa and pine boxes at a per unit cost of about $9. The promotion reflects the commitment of the studio to work all day and occasionally all night to get the job done.

These t-shirts were hand-delivered and mailed to retail clients who may have a need for clothing and/or point-of-purchase graphics. They also convey the studio's willingness to "work all day and into the night to get the job done."

Booklet created to raise awareness of the studio and invite existing and prospective clients, suppliers, photographers and illustrators to their fifth anniversary open house. The promotion plays off the studio's name and conveys, says David Butler, that "we're a fun place to visit and are right on the Missouri River." Three hundred were produced at a little over two dollars each. They were mailed in custom cardboard boxes with sawdust.

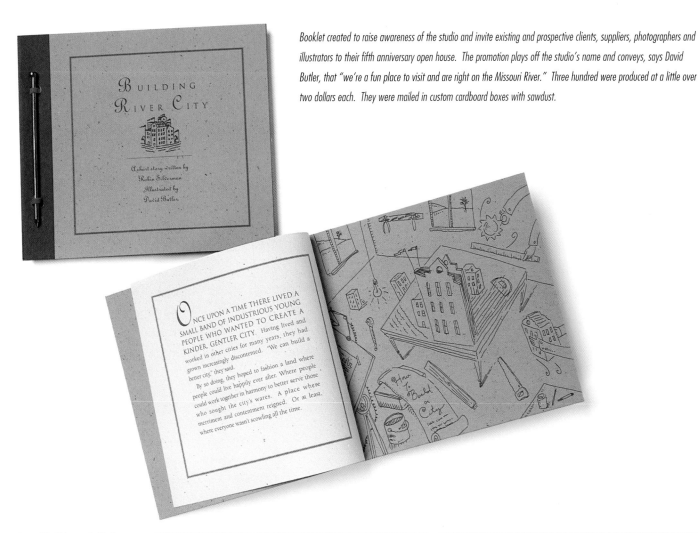

Created for Valentine Radford, a large advertising agency, to assure current and prospective clients that they wouldn't get lost in the shuffle or get snuffed out by a larger account, that they are, in fact, "big fishes." It was done as a very limited promotion and drew three new clients and approximately $3,000 in revenue.

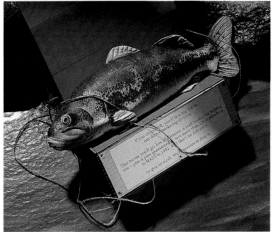

Client Mid-America Rehabilitation Hospital wanted to get doctors to refer patients to them. The tags on the skeleton are the key points doctors look for in rehabilitation hospitals. "We can put the pieces together," the hospital promotion says.

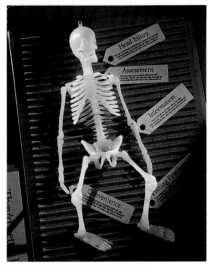

The promotions of the Pushpin Group are humorous, provocative, slightly outrageous, and they simply beg to be shared. As their two 1991 promotions impart, the group offers a variety of style and conceptual talent to match virtually any truth and emotion. "The Awful Truth" was designed by Seymour Chwast to imaginatively complement "a collection of right-minded quotations from our most honorable writers and raconteurs." It represents a perfect marriage of visuals and copy, as its slogans "Resist Hypocrisy and Pretense" and "Up with Veracity and Candor" cry out from the words and imagery on each page.

"What is Your Emotional Type?," which was initially inspired by eccentric typefaces, comic strips and poster art, ended up as a highly visual, oversized one-of-its-kind showcase—of everything from "aloof" and the style of Sergio Beradat to "zany" and the style of Seymour Chwast. Because the one-hundred-pound Trophy Dull Text paper was donated by Special Papers, the one-color book was especially low budget, at less than two dollars for each of the thirty-five hundred copies.

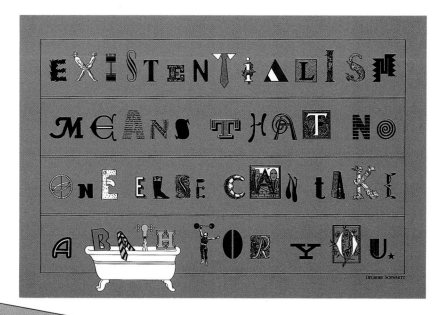

The idea for this promotion, designed by Seymour Chwast, came from a book of quotations entitled Friendly Advice, which he was asked to illustrate. In addition to unusual format, strong concept and design, and intriguing illustration, the 17" x 11 1/2" piece presents a highly creative use of paper stock and printing techniques.

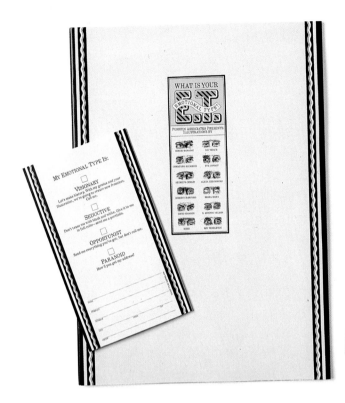

"What is Your Emotional Type?" was sent to art directors at magazines, book publishers, design firms and ad agencies. The promotion was received very well: Many response cards were mailed in, new illustrator portfolios were requested, and other Pushpin artists, with whom clients were already acquainted, received new assignments.

Bauhaus promotion, part of the "Design and Style" series presented by Mohawk Paper Mills and the Pushpin Group. It examines the relationship between printing technology and graphic style by looking at a particular historic design style and typography and its influence on contemporary graphic design. A large variety of Mohawk papers and printing techniques are stretched to their full potential by Pushpin's intelligent and provocative design.

When Southern California Lithographers opened a Northern California office, Lawrence Bender & Associates donated their services to get the word out to the Northern California market. The result is this vigorous display of the printer's capabilities, in which a very dense layer of ink was deftly applied to heighten the intensity of the color, four-color was used in the background to enhance the white's neutrality, and all eight colors (including the metallic colors and varnishes) were run in one press pass. Five thousand were produced at a cost of $10,000, and SCL is very pleased with the smart investment: The promotion resulted in at least twelve new customers and an estimated $300,000 in revenue.

Southern California
Lithographics
655 N. Tamarack Avenue
Brea
California 92621
(714) 529-0777
(800) 624-9292
FAX (714) 529-3018

Century City
Sales Office
2121 Avenue of the Stars
Suite 410
Los Angeles, CA 90067
(213) 284-7007
FAX: (213) 284-7060

With eight colors in one pass, you may begin to see things differently. We have the only eight-color Miehle Man-Roland press in t

Design:
Lawrence Bender
& Associates
Photography:
Mark Troutdale
Sunglasses courtesy of
SHADES, San Francisco

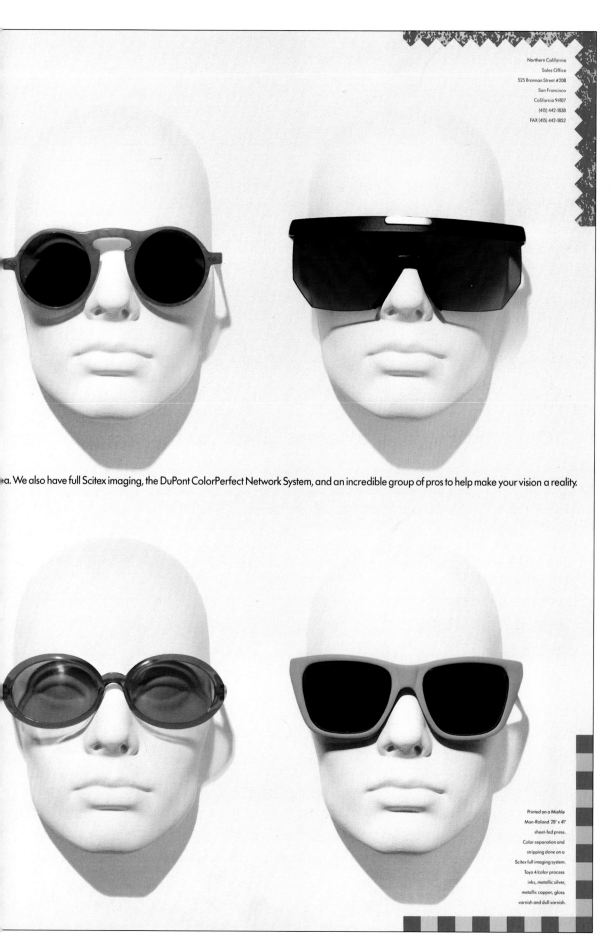

Northern California
Sales Office
525 Brannan Street #208
San Francisco
California 94107
(415) 442-1838
FAX (415) 442-1852

a. We also have full Scitex imaging, the DuPont ColorPerfect Network System, and an incredible group of pros to help make your vision a reality.

Printed on a Miehle
Man-Roland 28" x 41"
sheet-fed press.
Color separation and
stripping done on a
Scitex full imaging system.
Toyo 4/color process
inks, metallic silver,
metallic copper, gloss
varnish and dull varnish.

This promotion was profitable for the client as well as for Lawrence Bender. Of the one hundred phone calls he received in response, ten resulted in jobs that generated about $50,000 in income.

While on vacation in St. Croix, Mark Oldach and Janet Lorch eloped. When they returned to Chicago, they wanted to give family members, friends and colleagues the feeling of having been there with them on their wedding day, and they wanted to invite them to a grand old party to celebrate. So, Oldach designed this storybook, which humorously documents the development of their relationship, the ceremony in the Virgin Islands, and ends with: "So, like, do you wanna come to this party?" The story is one long run-on sentence, inspired, Oldach says, by "my wife's ability to talk without taking a breath." Each of the five hundred recipients called back, which makes Oldach wish they'd had an even bigger party.

Less personal and equally clever are the series of promotions the marketing communications firm has done for two of their printer clients. For both First Impressions and Active Graphics, Oldach took their names and ran, creating keen, attention-getting campaigns that build awareness and name recognition and communicate the printers' capabilities.

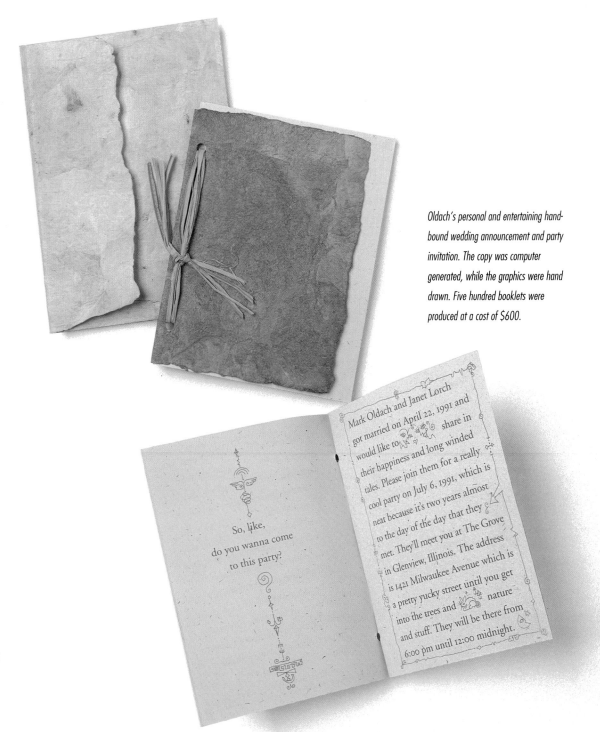

Oldach's personal and entertaining hand-bound wedding announcement and party invitation. The copy was computer generated, while the graphics were hand drawn. Five hundred booklets were produced at a cost of $600.

So, like,
do you wanna come
to this party?

Mark Oldach and Janet Lorch got married on April 22, 1991 and would like to share in their happiness and long winded tales. Please join them for a really cool party on July 6, 1991, which is neat because it's two years almost to the day of the day that they met. They'll meet you at The Grove in Glenview, Illinois. The address is 1421 Milwaukee Avenue which is a pretty yucky street until you get into the trees and nature and stuff. They will be there from 6:00 pm until 12:00 midnight.

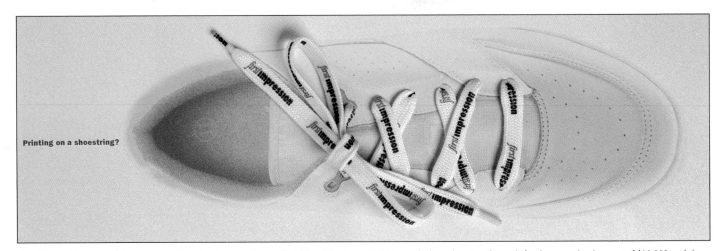

Printing on a shoestring?

One of a series of 15" x 4 3/4" postcards created to advertise the quality and affordability of First Impression Printers and Lithographers. Five thousand of each were produced at a cost of $10,000, excluding the printing. All pieces were printed at the same time, when the press was down, to save money. Following the mailing of each card, the company received a large influx of work.

To "activate a piece of paper through print, photography, design, typography and color technique," says Oldach, was the theme of the three-piece campaign for Active Graphics. Five thousand of each were mailed every four to six weeks to designers and other purchasers of four-color printing. The campaign generated sales of about $350,000.

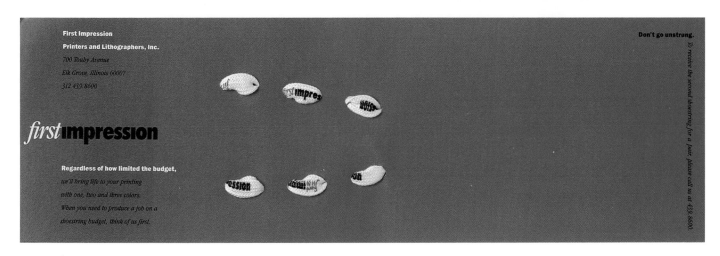

Bernard Maisner is the "Zelig" of hand lettering, a man with an extremely varied alphabet up his sleeve. As this frenzy of lettering illustrates, his talent ranges from the classic and traditional to the wild and crazy. He can imbue his letters with calm and sophistication or unharnessed emotion: the carefree gaiety emanating from a holiday greeting, the fiery anger of political revolt, the mix of determination and vulnerability expressed in the musical blues. Maisner hopes the editorial, publishing, advertising and television art directors who receive it as a direct-mail piece or see it in *American Showcase*, where it runs as an ad, will spend a good deal of time looking at and enjoying the piece. Then perhaps they will become inspired to use lettering for their projects and be introduced to options many do not think of when considering lettering.

Reproduced into six thousand postcards and one ad for American Showcase at under $1,000. The cost of the ad is about $3,500. Maisner used his rep Gerald & Cullen Rapp's mailing list.

The introduction of the first of this design firm's trademark books begins by saying that some of their best logos "were designed between eight p.m. and the ninth perfect idea." It goes on to say that every trademark is a separate puzzle for which the goal is to make a statement of identity. Little did they know then that this would lead to an annual addition to the series. Now at seven, each of the sixteen-page, saddle-stitched booklets presents two logos on each page, a direct and uncluttered showcase. Approximately five thousand of each book were produced at a cost of $8,000. They are mailed, as appropriate, to clients and new business prospects.

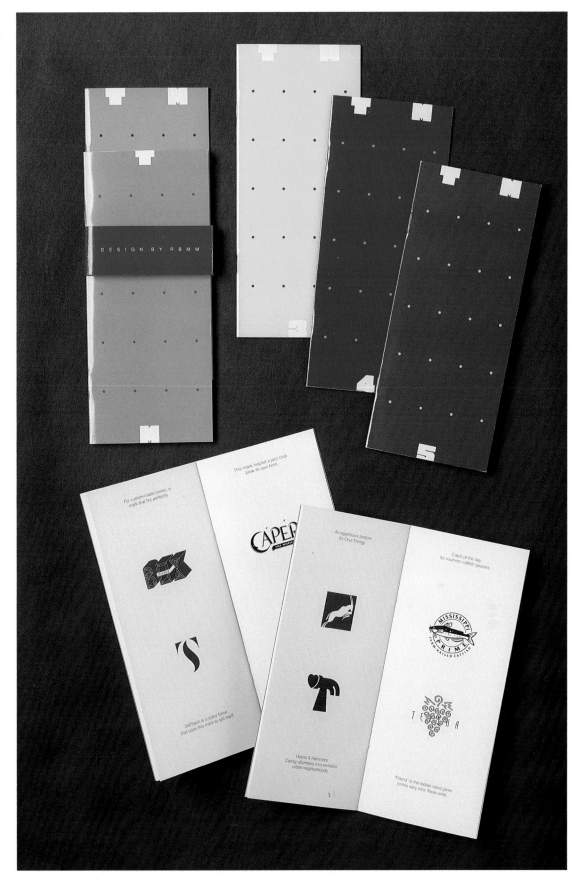

The design, layout and type of each were computer generated, output to Linotronic. Four match colors were used to differentiate each, while still managing to maintain a uniform look. The annual series was begun in 1983 to showcase the past year's trademark creations.

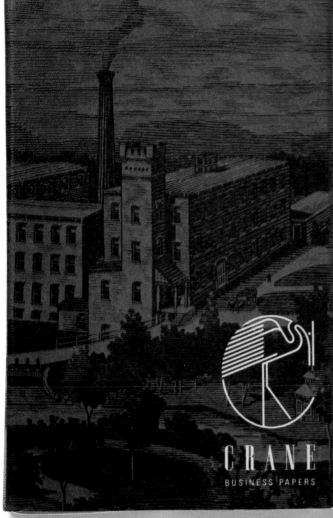

One of Chermayeff & Geismar's many corporate clients is Crane & Co, the only mill in the United States to manufacture 100 percent cotton fiber papers exclusively. As with anything of affordable quality, it often takes no more than one sip, one smell or one touch to convince one to buy the product. The studio's Crane notepaper box was created to do just this, to invite the potential buyer to try it out—touch it, feel the richness of pen pressed to paper. Resembling a large match box in design, the promotion also presents Crane's new identity and is practical in size.

The clever stamp campaign on the opposite page addresses the concern of many who feel that all-cotton fiber paper is too expensive for letterhead. As the campaign points out: Between 1917 and 1991, the postage rate multiplied by ten, and "now priced at twenty-nine cents for a one-ounce First Class letter, a little postage stamp is a big deal, and a four-cent Crane letterhead a better value than ever."

Seventy-five hundred notepaper boxes were sent to paper merchants, graphic designers, lawyers, stationery stores and distributors of Crane business papers. The piece was offset printed in two match colors, and thermography was used.

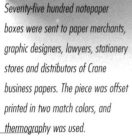

This conceptually direct and visually bold large-scale poster was offset printed in six color. The typography was done on the Macintosh. Ten thousand posters and fifty thousand mailers were mailed and handed out by sales reps.

When illustrator and portrait artist Stephen Alcorn says he has a "minimal" budget for self-promotion, he's not kidding. In fact, he paid not a cent for the production of each of the promotions on these pages. The poster to the right, which presents Alcorn's striking linocuts in rhythmic sequence, for example, was elegantly designed by the illustrator's father, John Alcorn, and produced in trade with Mohawk Paper Mills and Meriden-Steinham Press, both of which also used it as a promotion.

The idea for the handsome, full-color Lautrec calendar, Alcorn explains, was spurred by a recent discovery he had made regarding his printmaking—"that by printing light over dark and inverting the traditional cutting process, I could achieve a degree of fluidity and naturalism in my portraiture that is novel in the field of printmaking." Like Alcorn's other promotions, the piece was inspired by the artist depicted and sent to a variety of potential clients, primarily publishers.

Stowe / Uncle Tom's Cabin

Stendhal / The Red and the Black

D. H. Lawrence / Lady Chatterley's Lover

Thoreau / Walden Pond

James / The Portrait of a Lady

Walt Whitman

Hugo / Les Miserables

The Autobiography of Benvenuto Cellini

Henry Miller

Slave

Chopin / The Awakening

Byron / Don Juan

France / Penguin Island

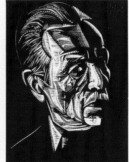

Edoardo DeFilippo

Crane / The Red Badge of Courage

Dickens / Bleak House

Stephen Alcorn / Linocuts

Printed by Meriden-Stinehour Press on Mohawk Superfine Cover, Regular Finish, White, basis 65

To promote two distinct approaches to portraiture Alcorn had developed in school, he created these simple, two-color, 14" x 22" posters, which he says, "made an extremely favorable impression on clients seeking portrait artists and drew many jobs." The paper was donated by Mohawk and the offset printing was done by Morgan Press.

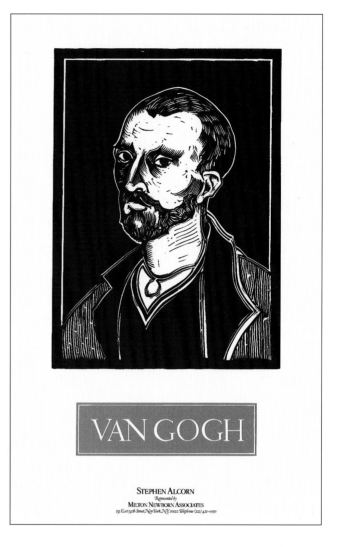

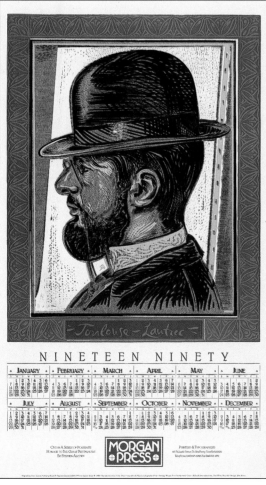

Morgan Press supplied the printing services, and John Alcorn, the illustrator's father, designed the piece. Three thousand of this one in a series titled "Portraits Homage to the Great Printmakers" were produced.

"The Bauhaus was my school of design," begins Primo Angeli in the preface to his book *Designs for Marketing.* The book offers chapter-by-chapter case studies of a range of his firm's projects—from the packaging of Henry Weinhard's and California Cooler to the identity system for the Asian Art Museum in San Francisco. They all communicate what grew out of Angeli's Bauhaus foundation, that which he terms "marketing design," an approach that involves balancing the concerns of aesthetics and sales. Also conveyed is the vast amount of work his firm has done for businesses in his beloved city of San Francisco, such as the packaging for Boudin Bread (sourdough French) and Lucca Delicatessens pasta. The city also figures prominently in Angeli's poster work, high-visibility design that is often created pro bono.

In celebration of the commercial and cultural Sister City exchange between San Francisco and Sydney, Australia, Angeli created the poster to the right, a vibrant limited edition for the "San Francisco Week in Sydney." He says, "I've always wanted to stick a giant olive on the TransAmerica building. After all, the martini, now a retrodrink, was a San Francisco tradition."

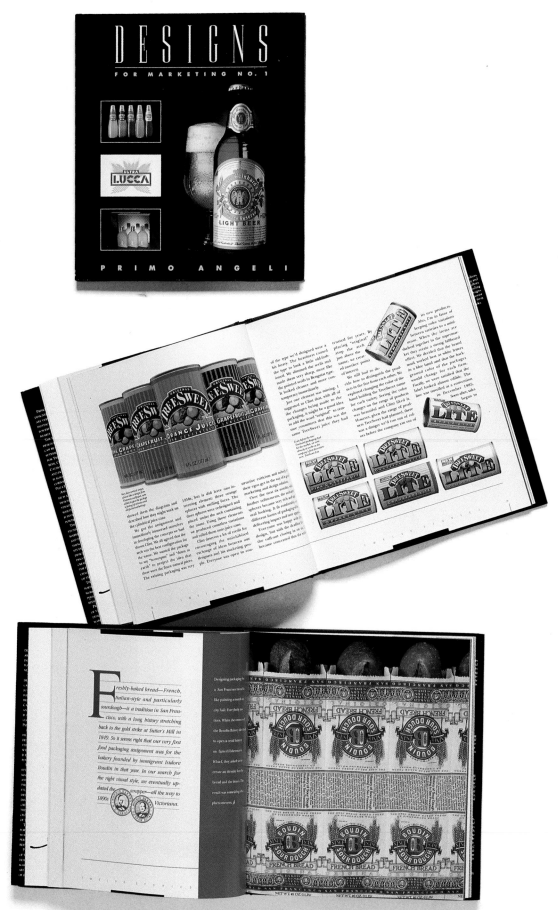

In his book Designs for Marketing, *Angeli explains on a case-by-case basis how several of his large-scale projects began and evolved. The 144-page book was published by Rockport Publishers.*

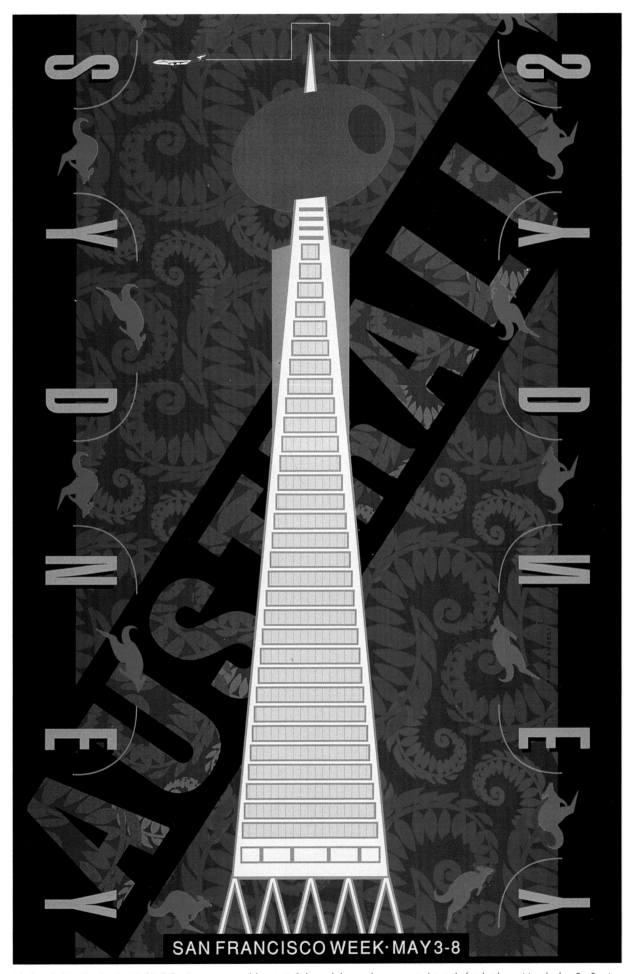

SAN FRANCISCO WEEK · MAY 3-8

This limited-edition "San Francisco Week in Sydney" poster announced the event in Sydney and also served as a memento. It touts the fact that the martini used to be a San Francisco tradition. Qantas Airlines was impressed and became a client. The Macintosh was used for type, layout, design, refinements and finished mechanicals.

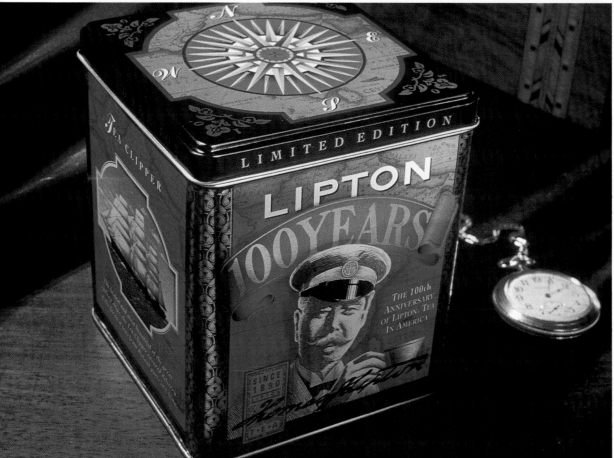

The flower reflects the cultural and Qantas Airlines (the kangaroo) reflects the commercial in this "Australia Week in San Francisco" poster. Five thousand were printed and three hundred were signed. As with Angeli's other poster work, it serves as an announcement as well as a collectible.

Angeli's objective here was to "create a distinctive one-hundred-year mark to be used on Lipton's entire line of products and create a new and unique collectible." One million were produced and sent to all corporate personnel and customers who buy Lipton products. Angeli's inspiration was "Sir Thomas Lipton and his great entrepreneurial American spirit."

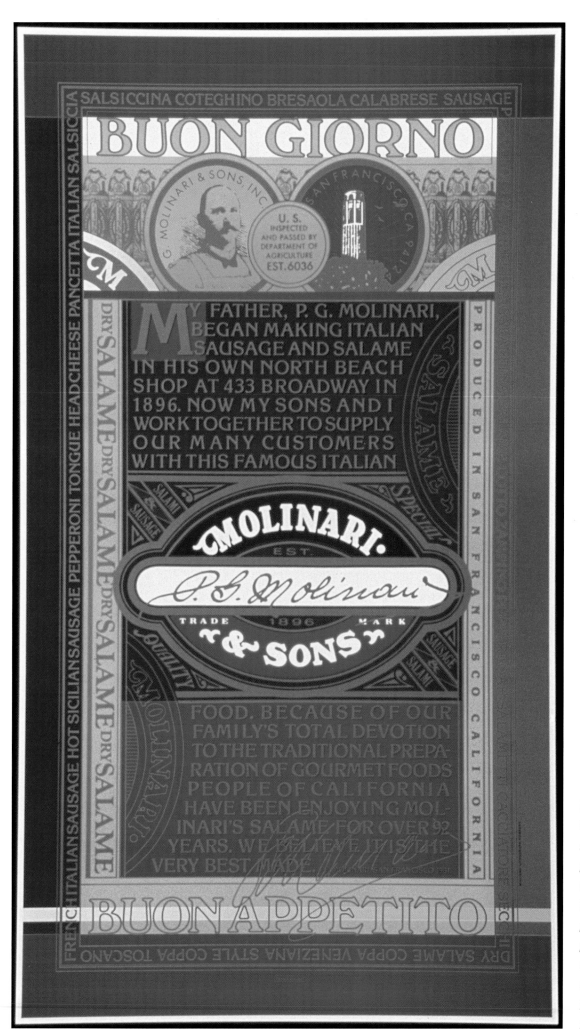

The Buon Giorno poster for Molinari & Sons was to be hung in prominent store locations and be a lasting promotion. Its design evokes a sense of the Molinari family's Italian heritage and their old world way of preparing food. The rich and ornate piece was very well received by the various delicatessens and meat distributors it was sent to and increased the design firm's visibility in the food design business.

Connie Helgeson-Moen's promotions are inexpensively created pieces that tout the fact that batik can be used as an innovative style of illustration. Both pieces were created in 1991 and are used as personal follow-ups or leave-behinds to portfolio showings, as well as direct mail. The above piece provides a hands-on sample of batik, the pattern of which coincides with her clever message: "The task of finding a new look in graphics can seem like a curse." But, "use a colorful style, not colorful language." She originally created one hundred booklets, at about seventy cents each, and puts together more as she needs them. It was such an economical piece, she explains, because "the booklet is handmade, with inexpensive materials. I modified the batik process to speed production and used grommets as a binding." The piece below was more expensive to produce at $350 for a limited edition of seventy. "It's still pretty new," Moen says, "but the publicity is promising."

Urging art directors to utilize her colorful style instead of the colorful language of frustration, the booklet offers a tactile sample of Moen's batik illustration. The inside text was computer generated and photocopied. The accordion folder shows various applications of batik as a medium. Costs were kept low by mounting color photocopies and using gold metallic pens for the type. Each was hand-assembled.

"After working at a newspaper," says Kathy Badonsky, "I never lost my attraction for strong, graphic, black-and-white editorial images and their more personal nature." Accentuating this sentiment is this pocket-sized, handmade book, which presents her artwork and rubber-stamped, spare copy in a small, yet powerful format. One is drawn into her work immediately by the die-cut cover, which reveals the first piece at a glance. Costs were kept down and quality up by using, says Badonsky, "the cleanest and blackest photocopy machine I could find in Atlanta." Rubber stamps were used to add another color. The promotion garnered positive comments about the intimate feeling of the book and brought in, estimates Badonsky, about 70 percent of her revenue for 1991. It has also resulted, she says, in work that is more creatively fulfilling.

Kathy Badonsky's small, 6" x 4 1/4", simple and tactile book was mailed to ten to fifteen designers and editorial art directors a week as they were produced. Next time, she says, she would handmake a larger number of books, and in addition, send out an enlarged copy of one piece—perhaps in poster form.

To exhibit to art buyers the work of the sixteen illustrators and six photographers he represents, James Conrad created a portfolio that he hoped would serve as a valuable resource in a creative reference library, with a shelf life of two to three years. It would, he envisioned, be "too good to throw away and too large to get lost in a file drawer." Each artist's distinctive work is placed in four color against a 16 ¹/₂" x 10 ¹/₂" background of dull-varnished white. To further reflect the distinctive style and sensibility of each artist, Conrad presents one quotation—from Jung to Lincoln—on each page, the content and typeface of which further communicate the quality and personality of each artist's work.

The translucent-plastic encased book is mailed out on an ongoing basis to art buyers at ad agencies, design studios, book publishers, editorial markets and corporate creative departments. Because of its loose format, it can easily be updated periodically. The production of two thousand cost $62,000.

Seventy-seven logos, each imbued with distinct individuality and allure, hang gracefully and regally in perfect balance, and, Margo Chase hopes—on the wall. The elegant poster was created, in part, for just this reason—the higher visibility the form offers, the fact that it is unlikely to get stuck in a drawer. The other characteristics of the poster worked in the studio's favor too: its immediacy in expressing the variety of logos they've designed, its self-explanation, and the ease with which it can be mailed. Result: Ten or so new projects from advertising agencies and other design studios (about $5,000 in revenue thus far), and, says Margo Chase, "hundreds of calls from students and other designers who wanted a copy."

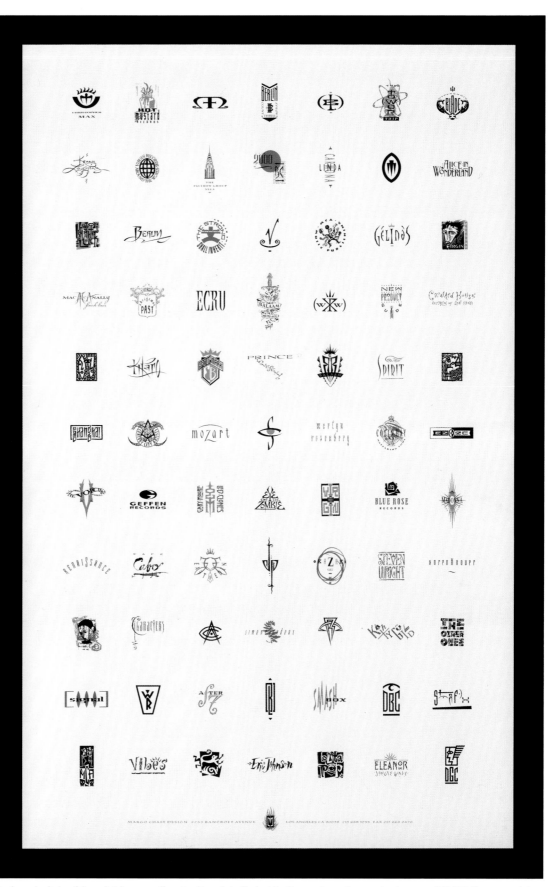

The three-color display of the studio's logos was offset printed in trade by Westland Graphics; two thousand were produced at a cost of $2,500. They were mailed in tubes to past and prospective clients and anyone who requested samples.

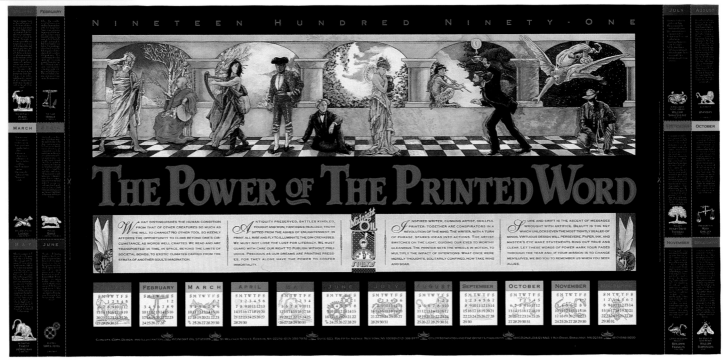

Produced in trade with the printer MacDonald and Evans. To save time and money, type was computer generated, output to Linotronic, and the original artwork was created the same size as its reproduction. While it is difficult for the studio to assess the amount of revenue it generated, creative director James M. Skiles says, it "has certainly paid for itself."

The longer one looks at Midnight Oil's 1991 promotional poster, the more one sees. Offering a celebration of the printed word, it presents a calendar, bookmarks for each month, and excerpts from the works of masters ranging from Plato to Joyce to Burroughs. In the background, intricate, twelve-color illustration presents such inspired creatives through the changing seasons of time. The studio used $20,000 of its $30,000 to $50,000 promotional budget for the production of four thousand pieces. While primarily intended as a holiday gift to clients, it was appropriate for year-round use.

The Stride Rite promotion evolved out of "a decade of familiarity with Stride Rite," says creative director James M. Skiles. The colorful and graphic poster was intended to appeal to both children and parents in promoting the seasonal purchase of footwear as an event.

Promotion for attendance at the MacWorld conference in general, and the Apple computer exhibits, more specifically; also an invitation to special V.I.P. MacWorld reception. Two thousand were produced for $15,000.

Approximately $15,000 was the cost of producing five hundred of this one of two posters sent to Stride Rite retail outlet stores. The silk-screened piece boosted Stride Rite's sales considerably.

For Webster Design's 1990 promotional project, the studio wished to present a range of their logo work and the degree to which their new computer skills have made them cost competitive in trademark design and thus, more attractive to middle-range companies that couldn't have afforded them in the past. They also desired to use up waste stock left over from a previous project. The ensuing creation is a 4 1/4" x 5", forty-two page, spiral-bound book. The presentation of one logo per page makes a strong statement on the depth of Webster's experience, and the foil-stamping, thermography and engraving on the cover begin the book with a bang. Despite the expensive techniques, the piece wasn't all that costly to produce. The printer wanted to use it as a promotion also, so the cover was done at half-rate. Type was produced on an in-house laser printer, and all type and logos were statted in-house. It worked very well for the studio, drawing twenty to thirty new projects and generating $25,000 to $35,000 in revenue.

Showcase of Webster Design's logo design. "From a marketing standpoint," says Dave Webster, "I feel name recognition and quantity is as important to our potential client as the quality of each piece." Quantity was emphasized by using one full page for each logo.

The theme of this promotional piece is "Get Your Business in Shape" with the latest technology from IBM. Unified with the stop watch, it inspires the decision-maker to "act now." All pre-press operations for the eight-color piece were computer generated, as well as the final film and negatives. Five hundred were produced for $8,500. It was distributed to companies that already own and use various IBM systems and was followed up with a phone call.

Inexpensive and unique business cards for an interior designer, which function as her complete marketing kit. When she completes a project, she incorporates the project's drapery material to make several business card swatches to provide her client with. The client is then able to use them to coordinate other elements of interior decorating and refer other people to the designer.

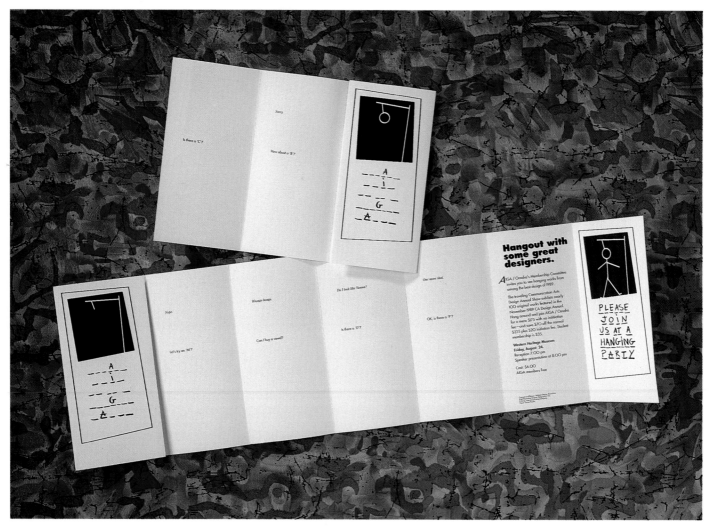

Webster's objective here was to design a promotion that would encourage people to join AIGA/Nebraska and come to a "Hanging Party" of some of the best graphic design in the country. It was simple and inexpensive to produce: forty cents per copy. The design, printing and paper were donated. "The paper was scrap from a previous job," Webster says. "That's why we used the unusual, long, horizontal format."

Daniel Baxter hoped the booklet promotion he created for corporate, educational, editorial and advertising clients would accomplish several things: offer a broad compilation of his drawings—"serious, humorous, and weird;" convey his strong conceptual skills—his ability to solve problems; and get hired as a result. "It is like a portfolio that art directors or designers can keep," he says, and because it's a booklet, it's "less likely to be thrown in the garbage." Fifteen hundred were designed, typeset and offset printed in one color at a cost of $1,100. The upshot was twenty-five new jobs, including "magazines I always wanted to get into, educational books, which I did all of the drawings for, my first advertising work," and $25,000 in generated revenue.

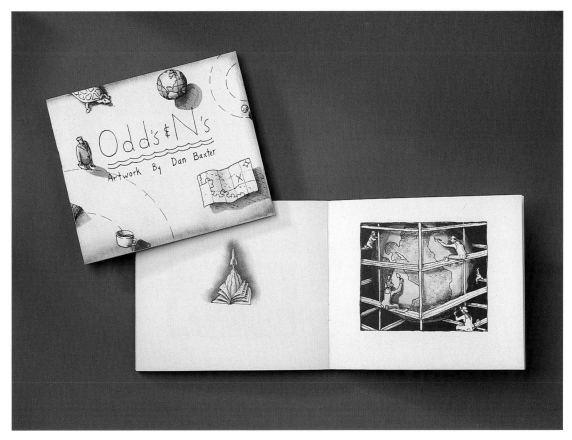

Twenty-page, 6" x 5" promotional booklet featuring Baxter's problem-solving ability. Less than a third of his self-promotion budget of $4,500 was spent on the production of fifteen hundred copies. Next time, Baxter says, he would list the assignment and client next to each image.

Four hundred of these direct-mail surrealist cards, inspired by the artist Archibaldo, were produced at a cost of fifty cents each. The two-color promotion was inexpensive because Baxter hired a printer who does only one- and two-color jobs, mostly business cards. The promotion brought Baxter eight new jobs and $5,000 in income.

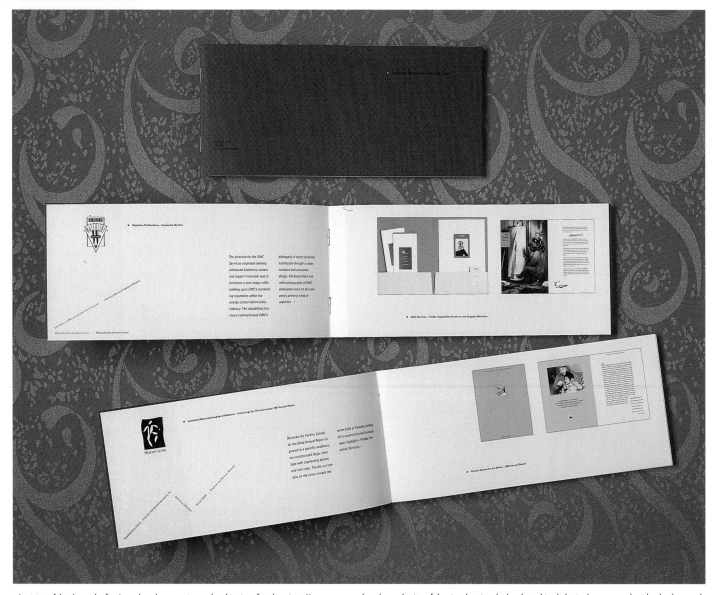

A mini-portfolio shows the firm's work and communicates the objective of each project. Money was saved on the production of the six-color piece by hand-punching holes in the cover stock with a leather punch and hammer and utilizing a format that fits in a cost-effective, standard envelope.

The promotions of Stewart Monderer Design convey the studio's complete range of graphic design services and the personality of its small-office environment. The professional and intimate 9" x 4" showcase of their past publications and identity projects, also communicating individual project objectives, serves as the studio's portfolio to potential clients. The straightforward, easy-to-read brochure, which cost a little over two dollars apiece, proved effective, resulting in eight new projects and an estimated $30,000 in revenue.

"In our search for themes and design directions for our holiday greeting," says designer Robert Davison, "we realized that many people don't have a place to go 'home' for food, family and warmth." In the spirit of the holiday season, they created a storybook-type greeting that revolves around the unfortunate problem of homelessness and heightens awareness of the growing problem. A large societal issue was successfully translated into the personal via the size and interrelation of type, color, illustration and copy.

Seven hundred fifty self-promotional holiday cards were produced at a cost of $2,000. In addition to demonstrating the studio's creative abilities, it addresses the social issue of homelessness through an exploration of what "home" means.

The Planet Design Company is clearly concerned with the goings-on of the planet—the political, the social and the cultural. Their promotions for such clients as the Madison AIDS Support Network, the American Players Theatre and the Madison Arts Center often include the large canvas of the poster, on which their images forcefully speak and the text elaborates. The intense and arresting screen print done for the Madison AIDS Support Network conveys anguish, determination and support, and successfully brought awareness to the cause and the group. The design was donated; the typesetting and printing amounted to $250 for three hundred copies.

For the American Players Theatre, Dana Lytle and Kevin Wade designed and Erik Johnson illustrated a poster and schedule to generate ticket sales for the 1991 season. With vibrancy, simplicity and classical type, the concept of "Shakespeare in the Woods" conveys the sense of enjoyable theater in a natural setting. The set was mailed to renewal subscribers and is estimated to have generated $200,000 in revenue for the internationally renowned classical theater.

Screen print designed pro bono for the Madison AIDS Support Network. Three hundred were mailed to volunteers and displayed publicly. The piece was done inexpensively by using tagboard as a third color. It brought much needed attention to the group and the disease and resulted in a great many write-ups and awards for the studio.

Five thousand of both the American Players Theatre poster and schedule were designed and produced for $25,000. The design, layout and type were done on the computer through Linotronic. The pieces were offset printed in five match colors.

...YOU WILL HEAR UNCONTROLLABLE *laughter* AND GROUPS OF PEOPLE WEEPING WITH *joy*. DIGNIFIED WOMEN WILL *scream* AT THE TOP OF THEIR LUNGS. WELL-DRESSED BUSINESSMEN WILL FALL TO THEIR KNEES, *whispering* STRANGE INCANTATIONS. SOME WILL *jump* OUT OF THEIR SEATS, OTHERS WILL *flail* THEIR ARMS *wildly* IN THE AIR, WHILE OTHERS WILL *pound* ONE ANOTHER ON THE BACK WITH *great force*. THESE BEHAVIORS CAN BE WITNESSED SEVERAL TIMES A DAY AT APPROXIMATELY *22-minute intervals*. DO NOT BE ALARMED. AS STRANGE AS THEY MAY SEEM, THESE SAME *rites and rituals* TAKE PLACE EVERYDAY HERE AT THE TRACK. WE ASSURE YOU NONE OF THESE PRACTICES WILL SEEM THE SLIGHTEST BIT *unusual* AFTER YOU'VE PLACED YOUR FIRST $2.00 bet.

THE MANAGEMENT

WARNING:
WHAT YOU SEE AND HEAR TODAY MAY
AT FIRST SHOCK AND AMAZE YOU...

The rites and rituals of the race track, the secrets of picking winners, "how to bet like the big boys," and the mysteries of the tote board are some of the things revealed in this colorful and unusual brochure for new enthusiasts of Arlington Race Track. The 6 ½" x 14" six-color brochure cost $60,000 to design, typeset and print. The twenty-one thousand copies were either sold or given away at the track.

To promote the Eleanor Moore modeling agency, Planet Design created this visually striking catalog, which combines strong duotone and tritone photography with simple design. The studio, photographer and printer gave discounts in exchange for credit lines. The final production cost was one dollar each for five thousand copies. It was mailed to art directors, designers and photographers—those on the lookout for models. It has drawn two new fashion and life-style clients for Planet Design.

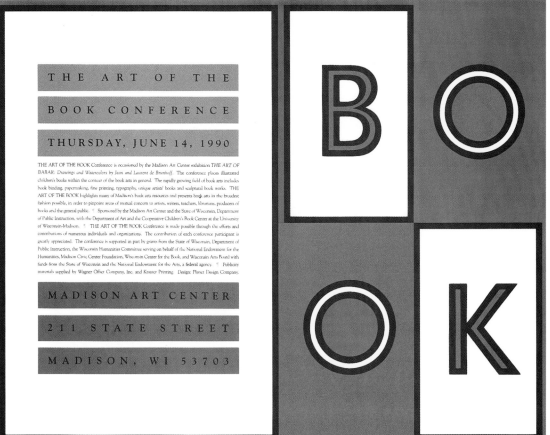

THE ART OF THE

BOOK CONFERENCE

THURSDAY, JUNE 14, 1990

THE ART OF THE BOOK Conference is occasioned by the Madison Art Center exhibition *THE ART OF BABAR: Drawings and Watercolors by Jean and Laurent de Brunhoff*. The conference places illustrated children's books within the context of the book arts in general. The rapidly growing field of book arts includes book binding, papermaking, fine printing, typography, unique artists' books and sculptural book works. THE ART OF THE BOOK highlights many of Madison's book arts resources and presents book arts in the broadest fashion possible, in order to pinpoint areas of mutual concern to artists, writers, teachers, librarians, producers of books and the general public. ❦ Sponsored by the Madison Art Center and the State of Wisconsin, Department of Public Instruction, with the Department of Art and the Cooperative Children's Book Center at the University of Wisconsin-Madison. ❦ THE ART OF THE BOOK Conference is made possible through the efforts and contributions of numerous individuals and organizations. The contribution of each conference participant is greatly appreciated. The conference is supported in part by grants from the State of Wisconsin, Department of Public Instruction, the Wisconsin Humanities Committee serving on behalf of the National Endowment for the Humanities, Madison Civic Center Foundation, Wisconsin Center for the Book, and Wisconsin Arts Board with funds from the State of Wisconsin and the National Endowment for the Arts, a federal agency. ❦ Publicity materials supplied by Wagner Offset Company, Inc. and Kramer Printing. Design: Planet Design Company.

MADISON ART CENTER

211 STATE STREET

MADISON, WI 53703

This poster's design and use of classic typefaces reflect the aesthetic of books and inform the audience about an educational conference on book arts. One thousand were produced at a cost of $5,000. The two-color, offset-printed self-mailer was sent to universities, educational institutions, libraries, museums, and those on the sponsoring Madison Art Center's mailing list. It drew many to the conference and more poster assignments to the studio.

Four-color poster designed by Kevin Wade and Dana Lytle. It was inspired by spring and conceived to draw attention to an event at the Madison Art Center in which floral art interacts with the center's permanent collection. Two thousand copies of the memorable and framable work were sent to those on the Center's mailing list or displayed publicly.

The Graphic Expression has a knack for presenting an image of their corporate clients that is conservative yet contemporary. At the core of their success is their ability to present their corporate clients as though they are genuinely and proudly speaking for themselves. Dillon, Read & Co., Inc., the major international full-service investment banking firm, is one such client. For the company's 1990 annual report, The Graphic Expression used simple and direct design, an assortment of textured paper, and full-page bleed illustrations in a variety of styles to convey the firm's investment service capabilities, as well as the people behind them.

The firm's real estate brochure introduces the capabilities of this department to real estate investors and developers by displaying the company's past expertise through large, crisp, full-color photographs of some of these projects.

This annual review brochure was produced for Dillon, Read & Co., Inc. at a cost of about $12 a copy. The design was computer generated, and it was reproduced in six color.

Three thousand of this capabilities brochure were produced for $70,460. It was mailed to potential investors in real estate projects.

Scott Hull's 1990 and 1991 promotions for the top American illustrators he represents spring from strong concepts that humorously tap into the joys and agonies of design. They are, in effect, illustrated guides: "Facing the Annual Report," "Surviving the Creative Process," and "Design Tools Through History." They spur art directors to read them from start to finish and offer a playful and conceptually invigorating forum for these artists to strut their stuff—their abilities to respond to a creative problem with their own unique visions. About "Design Tools Through History," Hull says, "Early returns show our efforts have paid off for all participants. Everyone is buzzing about the top-shelf promotion. It's a real keeper."

Joint promotion for design firm, printing company and Scott Hull Associates. All services were donated to the production of twenty-five thousand copies. For most designers the annual report is a dream project. By explaining, step-by-step, the annual report process, the promotion explains in conceptual illustration on a background of seven match colors that the process can also be a nightmare.

▶ *Each of the illustrators represented by Scott Hull has a singular vision of a segment of design history. Each is able to show it in this weaving together of two stories—a light-hearted observance of the origin of each design tool, accompanied by a description of the artist's own creative process. Fifteen thousand of the spiral-bound book were mailed and handed out to ad agencies, design firms, publishers, editorial and in-house corporate clients.*

"Surviving the Creative Process" takes a look at every part of it—dealing with the client, staying afloat, playing hurry-up-and-wait, and reaping the rewards. Some forty-five thousand were distributed throughout the year. Because of the large distribution, says Hull, the calls are still coming in.

The clean, simple format of this eight-inch square brochure neatly presents the contemporary yet classic, textured illustration of Greg Dearth. The promotion, Hull says, "set Greg apart from other artists doing scratchboard," resulted in phone calls—("too many to count"), and "doubled Greg's income."

GENE SASSE, INC.
POMONA, CALIFORNIA

Photographer Gene Sasse is a master of light, shadow and form. His artful work allows the viewer to connect so well with the image that one never senses Sasse's presence. Since 1988 he has presented this mastery in calendar form, in joint promotion with the separator, Fox Colour, and the printer, Premier Printing Corporation. Each year fifteen hundred are sent to designers, architects and ad agencies. The 1990 calendar "Natural Light" is a result of Sasse's desire to photograph more landscapes in black and white. The piece was well received and resulted in a calendar project for Pomona College, as well as a book entitled *Natural Thought*. Sasse estimates the calendar brought $10,000 in income.

New Mexico was the inspiration for his 1991 calendar, which conveys the variety and flavor of the Southwest region. "The background wall," Sasse explains, "was constructed to give the feeling of an adobe wall. A white card was raised off the background to cast a shadow so the photographs appear suspended in front of the wall." The background separations were made from one original, and the color bars at the top were changed electronically using a Crossfield Imaging System.

1990 and 1991 four- and six-color calendars were created as joint promotions for photographer Gene Sasse, separator Fox Colour and printer Premier Printing Corporation. Each calendar uses handsome design, distinctive typography and complementary quotations to enhance the flavor of the images. Each has been well received and lead to many new projects for Sasse.

John Sayles entered the world of university rush design when Sheree Clark worked at Drake University and was responsible for fraternity and sorority promotion. She found the existing pieces "abominable" and thought it would be wise to hire a designer. She went to John Sayles. Shortly thereafter, the two joined forces and have been doing rush promotions ever since. Like the poster for Cal State University Fullerton, they are meant to encourage new students to register for rush and are mailed to their homes during the summer. Concepts arise from the particularities of place as well as the objectives and offerings of the Greek system. This CSUF rush promotion uses waves to appeal to its Southern California audience, an image that also underscores the idea of "jumping in" to the college scene via the Greek system and making a "splash" when one gets to college. While the rush projects are not high profit, they offer the studio the chance to transcend the constraints of a committee and "men in pinstripe suits," says Clark.

Designed to get students to register for rush at Cal State University Fullerton, the two-color poster was conveniently folded into a self-mailer and sent to three thousand new students during the summer. The original artwork was done by John Sayles in black charcoal. The softness resulted from it being printed entirely in pastel inks on a lilac-colored paper stock.

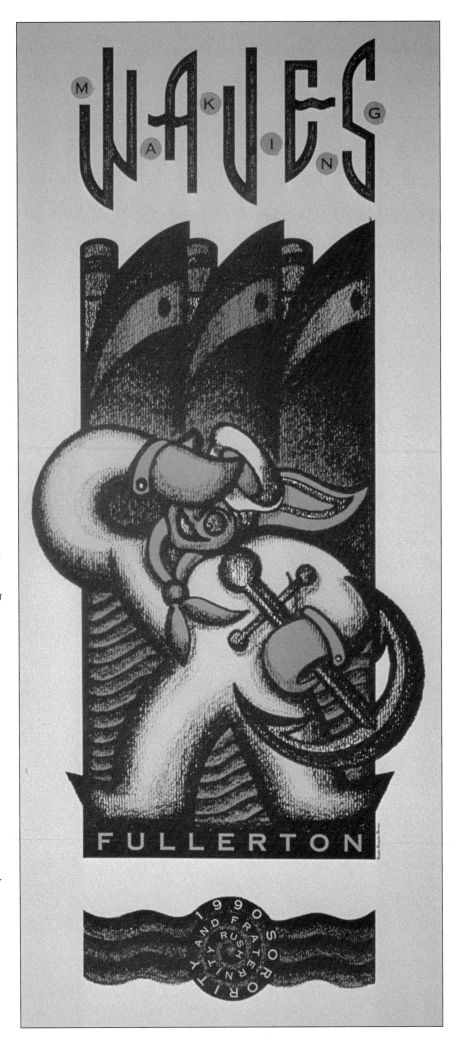

Unified under the title "We've Got the Beat on Greek Street," this Drake University fraternity and sorority summer mailing and on-campus promotion is an integrated use of many media—audio (a customized two and one-half minute tape), print, display and textiles.

The success of this campaign for Gettysburg College's rush is, says Sheree Clark, that "it's bright, upbeat and attention-getting—important criteria for an on-campus promotion. It's also become its own premium: People wanted the paint can, even if they weren't interested in rush." Six hundred of the cans and brochures were produced and handed out. One hundred of the posters were printed and hung on campus. A split fountain technique was used to save money in the printing process.

Greek life was positioned as a "basic" at Northwestern University, hence the theme "Building Blocks for Success." An attention-getting square box was mailed with interior die-cut brochure that has protruding sections or "blocks." Two thousand were mailed out to the university's new students.

Sent to new male students at U.C. Berkeley to encourage them to sign up for fraternity rush. Taking their cue from the client's determined theme of "Build Your Future," the design firm opted for an industrial look: The silk-screened cover of the self-mailing is corrugated cardboard and the saddle-stitch is industrial staples. The integrated campaign, in addition to the main brochure, includes letterhead, staff t-shirt and rush "guidebook."

Many of the promotions of Walter Neals Design are clever replications of various products. The packaging of the coffee promotion for Newtrend, for example, a company which provides software, technology and professional services to the financial industry, looks very much like it belongs in a specialty store. Created to promote Newtrend's exhibit at a national trade show, the package was mailed to media, to registered show delegates, and to seven thousand prospects in the target market prior to the event. About $14,000 was spent on the promotion, which, in addition to coffee, coffee cakes and a mug, contained notice of how to register to win a trip to a Jamaican coffee plantation. It succeeded in attracting traffic to the exhibit and interesting the media. It brought in several new clients for Newtrend, amounting to several hundred thousand dollars in revenue.

Appealing to a smaller audience and setting an altogether different mood was the "Labyrinth of Passion" invitation to a Valentine's Day mystery ball. The eighteenth-century love letter-lookalike was inspired by the films *Dangerous Liaisons* and *Cyrano de Bergerac*.

The packaging labels and cards were illustrated and lettered by hand and offset printed in four color. The image was screen printed onto the mugs. The promotion piqued interest in Newtrend's exhibit at a national trade show convention, heightened recognition of the company, and is estimated to have brought several hundred thousand dollars in revenue.

Conveying romance and passion, the invitation was mailed to about three hundred fifty patrons of the theater and ballet companies. The cost of the two-color invitation was about $400. It brought two hundred guests to the event and generated an estimated $8,000.

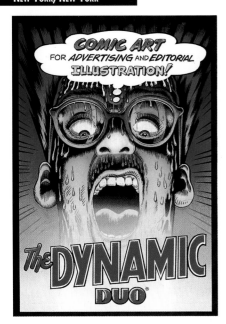

The objective for the Duo's self-promotional postcard is "to get art directors and buyers to notice our work and hire us," Schumer says. Each postcard was treated like a comic book panel, and a personalized message to each art director appeared on the back.

The work of this advertising and editorial illustration studio is bright, bold and dynamic—it is comics, after all. Simple presentation in comic strip fashion, with high-quality reproduction is what seems to work best for their promotions. Almost their entire workload comes from their annually new and improved ad in *American Showcase*, which generates an estimated $100,000 for the studio each year. Another mode of self-promotion for them is a series of postcards, which are mailed to current and prospective clients. The cost is shared with the studio's art rep, Gerry Rapp.

Recently released by Chronicle Books is *Visions From the Twilight Zone*, a book by the Duo's Arlen Schumer that treats "Twilight Zone" images as black-and-white art photography, showing that both the show and the art form were influenced by twentieth-century surrealist art and subsequently influenced the modern art that followed them. With a cover that resembles a miniature television, Schumer designed the long accordion strip with strong black-and-white graphics to invite members of the New York City Art Directors Club to the multimedia presentation based on his book. Three thousand were produced for $1,500.

"Whereas most illustrators plunk down their work down on the page to advertise themselves," says Schumer, "I design our pages to make them stand out from the crowd, and it is a crowd," he says. The double-page spread in American Showcase resulted in twenty to forty jobs for the studio.

Schumer's invitation shows, he says, "black-and-white television images in a fresh way, so that it might entice art directors to come see them live." It seems it did because the Art Director's Club was filled to capacity. Schumer is pleased that as a result of the show, two writers are working on articles inspired by the show, one of which is for the New Yorker.

The form of Ellen Hall's promotions evolved out of her determination that her business card and resumé not be drowned in the "sea of mail" art directors are forced to contend with each day. Rather, she set out to create something that would rise to the surface, be interactive, memorable, and display her strength in conceptual design. Intent upon creating a flipbook for a business card, she happened upon an image of a clown, and the circus theme was born. Next would be the "animal cracker" resumé, for which animals were carefully chosen to best represent each area of her background. The pride of a lion, for example, was used to represent "awards." The response to the pieces, which were mailed together, was one of "delight," says Hall: several dozen phone calls, two freelance jobs with ad agencies, and an additional income of $1,200. The pieces were very inexpensively produced due to the amount of work she did by hand—coloring, cutting and assembling; and because she used a rubber stamp for her phone number, none of the pieces will need to be reprinted if she moves.

Two hundred of each piece were offset printed in one color. The production costs were $100 for the stationery, $250 for the flipbook, and $300 for the "animal cracker" resumé. The pieces were mailed together in a larger box to art directors at ad agencies and design studios in the San Francisco Bay area two to three times a week.

Villa's letterpressed card series conveys her conceptual talent and communicates something about Villa. The dog image was done for Valentine's Day; the hand, she says, "is a spiritual image about the use of my hands and my perception combined with outside forces;" the third is a self-portrait communicating her conceptual (cerebral) abilities.

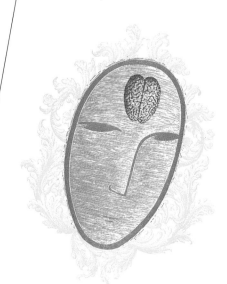

Roxana Villa has her very own letterpress, a Vandercook Universal One Proof Press, and has named it "Permanent Press." In addition, she has an assortment of engravings, dingbats and other items that she loves to find ways of combining with her scratchboard illustration. To generate interesting, conceptual illustration jobs as well as create interest in her work, she sends her images out on simple and effective 5" x 7" cards. She also prints them on stickers, which are placed on envelopes and packages to garner immediate attention. About the cards, she says, "they always attract a lot of interest. Art directors see them as gems compared to slick four-color cards. I think they view them as more personal than standard promotions." The production of two hundred fifty of each card runs about $100; the individual illustrations are usually reused on other promotions. The "cerebral" card, for example, was used on her letterhead as well as on a sticker.

ROXANA VILLA • 105 MONTAGUE STREET • BROOKLYN, NEW YORK • 11201

Two hundred stickers were produced for $75 and are meant to be, says Villa, "a quick way to show my work and entice the viewer." She says a whole package containing a tearsheet, other samples of her work, and stickers have increased her work load by about 60 percent.

The new digs of Samata Associates are in none other than an old bowling alley. To celebrate the firm's grand reopening, they felt it fitting to present an invitation and commemorative decoration in the form of the old pins themselves. Three hundred fifty of them were speckle-printed, tagged, packaged and mailed to clients, associates, suppliers and friends at a total cost of $5,000.

On a more subdued note is the 1991 brochure that promotes the firm's annual report services. The sophisticated and confident brochure begins by emphasizing that an annual report must have a positive impact and cause the reader to come away with a clear and accurate understanding of the depicted corporation and its strategies. The firm then proceeds to show by doing: it offers a sampling of their past year's annual report jobs on a project-by-project basis. Each page exhibits the cover, striking photograph or illustration, and copy that explains what they did and why. In the end the recipient knows just how Samata would be able to satisfy their annual report needs. So perhaps it is not surprising that the firm is now doing Fortune 500 annual reports.

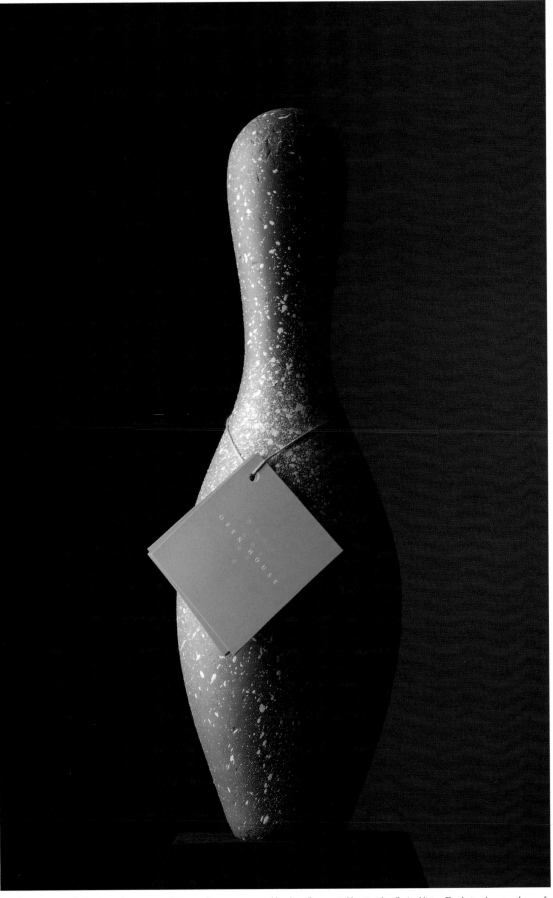

Novelty invitation to the firm's grand reopening at their new offices—a renovated bowling alley—suitably using the alley's old pins. The design, layout and type of the tags were computer generated.

For this showcase of a year's worth of the firm's annual report work, production costs of the six-color piece ran $12,000 for eight thousand copies. It went to a target audience of annual report buyers. What has emerged thus far are fifty phone calls, about five new clients, and Fortune 500 annual report projects.

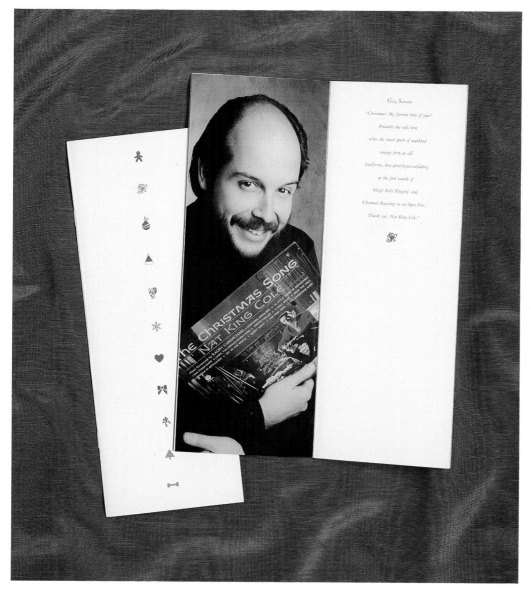

Holiday greeting brochure, the theme of which is the favorite Christmas memories of Samata employees. The sentimental piece offers insight into the staff on a personal level and emphasizes each individual's working style. It was sent to current clients.

Vaughn/Wedeen's 1990 gift to current and prospective clients. It was delivered in person when possible, otherwise by mail. The promotion drew one new client and many new projects, several of which were in packaging.

Vaughn/Wedeen's holiday gifts convey their print design capabilities while also offering thanks for the creative opportunities their current and prospective clients present them with each year. To share their love of design and fondness for certain local products, the studio created strong and colorful identities for these Christmas promotions that are carried from one piece to the next without becoming static. The layout and type of the food labels were done on computer, output to Linotronic, and were printed in four match and four process colors in donation from Albuquerque Printing. The image on the labels exhibits, says designer Dan Flynn, the designers' pleasure at being able to work amidst New Mexico's beautiful surroundings. To economize, the labels were printed on one stock, and, explains Flynn, "the whole firm chipped in and put all of the crates together." One hundred fifty of them were created for about $19,500.

"Santa's Private Reserve," the firm's 1989 gift. Vaughn/Wedeen employees selected the wine and helped with assembling the boxes and labeling the bottles. In most cases, the gifts were delivered in person. Six match colors were used on the offset-printed labels. The package drew several new projects for the firm.

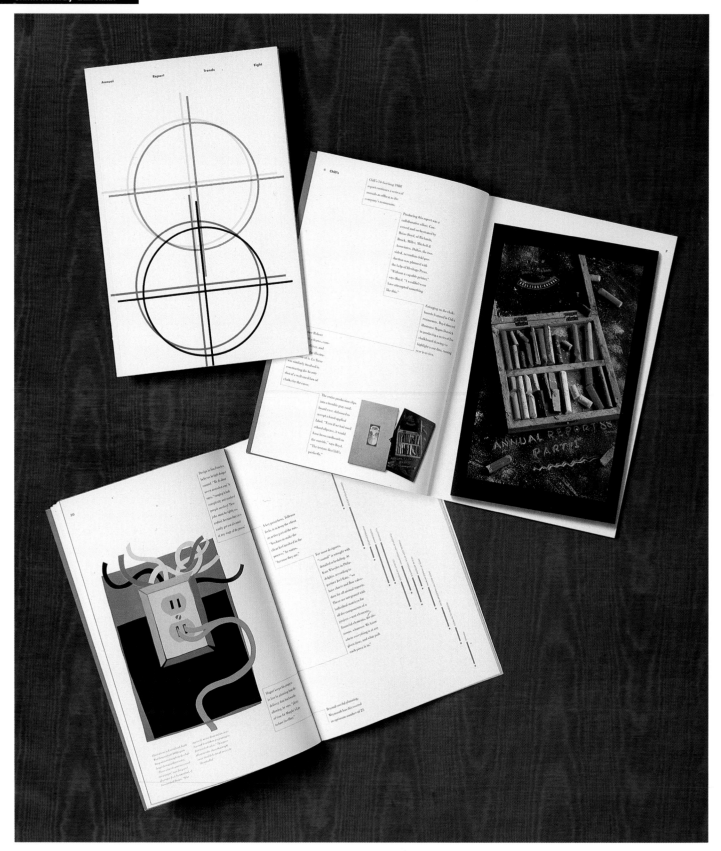

One hundred fifty thousand copies of the high-profile, six-color "Annual Report Trends Eight" were sent to paper specifiers, art directors, designers, printers, corporations and other buyers of fine paper.

The S.D. Warren Company commissioned John Cleveland, while he was at Bright & Associates, to design a brochure that would reveal trends and excellence in annual report design. The result is this crisp and arresting perfect-bound book. Through sophistication of style, clarity of execution, excellence in reproduction, and the fine writing of Rose DeNeve, it presents a series of five unique annual report case histories, a designer discussion about how to get the best from clients and printers, and a look at three trends within graphic design. It's a blend that amounts to an exceptional promotion for S.D. Warren.

R.M. Schneider's illustration brochure is smart. It shows his style and clear and practical thought about a range of subject matters—in a format appropriate to both the corporate and editorial markets it was mailed to. "I wanted the art directors," Schneider explains, "to have a permanent booklet, not just a single sheet, to refer to when they were looking for an illustrator. I tried to emulate the *American Showcase* books, but make it only for myself. This book provides the art director with one-stop shopping." Its size is large enough to show the sharp detail of seven past projects, yet it is small enough to fit into a file drawer. Twenty-five hundred of the four-page, saddle-stitched booklet were produced at a cost of $2,200. The strategy paid off for Schneider, for he was awarded with sixteen new clients and six different types of projects, which included advertising assignments and trade show graphics. He estimates the brochure drew $28,000 in revenue.

Schneider's 7" x 11" corporate and editorial illustration brochure printed in four process colors and varnish on the printer's house paper stock. Four brochures were printed on each press sheet. There are two things Schneider wishes he had done differently: "Add more pages and print twice the amount."

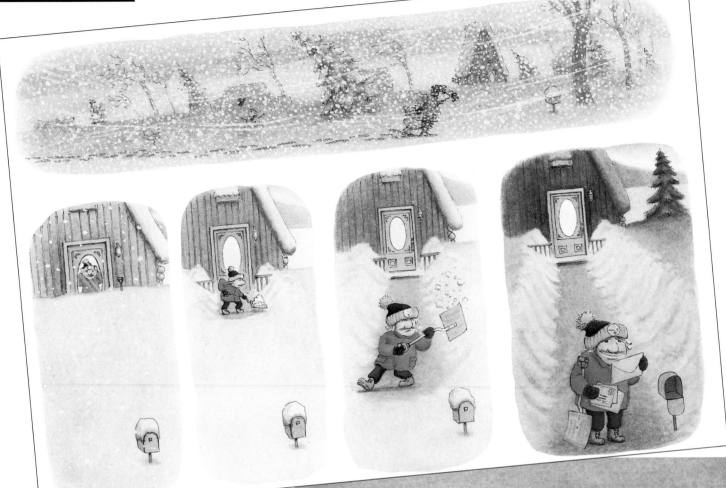

When Jeff Moores moved from the urban cacophony of New Jersey to the tranquility of the western New York country, the themes of his promotions and Christmas cards changed. The sequential storyteller left subways, traffic jams and other big-city frustrations behind and embraced his new abode's less hectic pace and unique discomfitures. His first Christmas card here conveys a more relaxed, longer-haired guy than in previous Moores cards as he contends with what can happen in Snow Belt country. Two thousand were produced at a cost of $3,000.

The "Be Different" theme originated from a *Newsweek* assignment Moores did in May of 1990 about younger siblings and their tendency to be the most innovative members of the family. The simple design has lead to many assignments thus far, including a couple of ads for *People* magazine, a promotional campaign for a cardiology firm, and thirteen detailed illustrations for T.C.B.Y.'s 1992 calendar. The concept has unlimited possibilities, and "since we've recently had our first baby," he says, "I'm inspired daily by my son, Charlie."

Moores' first Christmas card, depicting his new rural life in western New York. While city life presents its own set of frustrations, so too can life in the country, especially in the Snow Belt. As a result of the card, Moores received a few full-page spread assignments.

Two in a series of four "Be Different" postcards. One thousand of each were produced at a total cost of $600. They were mailed to ad agencies, design studios and magazines.

Moving announcement for the firm's clients and suppliers, a humorous variation on a classic poem. Two hundred of the two-color pieces were produced at a cost of $700. "It was right on the money in describing our experience," says Eric Rickabaugh, "and at the same time, it entertained the audience."

"Twas the night before moving when all through the house, nothing was packed, not even the mouse." So begins Rickabaugh Graphics' moving announcement, a take-off on the well-known Christmas poem. Accompanying the Clement Moore-based verse is a humorous portrayal of their moving experience and 1950s imagery. The booklet waxes nostalgic, which is something Rickabaugh does quite well and often. A similar tone is set with their use of rubber stamps to convey a distinctive Rickabaugh sign-off on all items sent to clients and suppliers. The stamps serve, says the public relations-wise Eric Rickabaugh, "to remind our clients continuously of the value of creative ideas."

So does DesignWorks, their in-house retail space, intended to expose the local community to their designs. Sold in the shop are rubber stamps, t-shirts and posters. The packaging, along with the interior decor of the shop, projects a 1950s, industrial, blue-collar image.

Designed by Eric Rickabaugh and John Smith for staff use on correspondence and packages. At a cost of five dollars each, they give an inexpensive and creative touch to even the simplest letter. Since the firm has always played with rubber stamps, it seemed time to create their own.

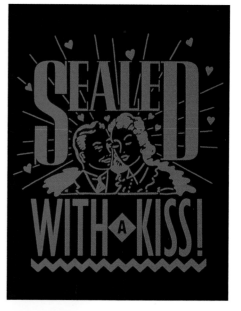

Rubber stamps created for sale in the firm's DesignWorks shop, a retail space in which their design is made available to the local community. The novel and utilitarian stamps were inspired by the firm's huge collection of 1950s advertising art. Fifty were produced at a cost of five dollars each.

Some of the products sold in DesignWorks. The packaging, via kraft paper and black-and-cream inks, is meant to reinforce the industrial, blue-collar, fun and tongue-in-cheek image of the shop. The packaging required no die-cuts, scores or other special production techniques, and all labels were designed to require minimal labor to apply.

The retail installations of DesignWorks. Their approximate cost was $4,000. The faux-steel pipes and riveted panels strengthen the desired "look" of the shop.

Commemorative poster for the five-hundredth anniversary of Columbus's "discovery" of America, a great interest for them locally because many of the year's celebrative events will be held in Columbus. All services were donated and copies of the poster were used by all parties as a promotional tool. It was sent to clients and used as a leave-behind for potential ones.

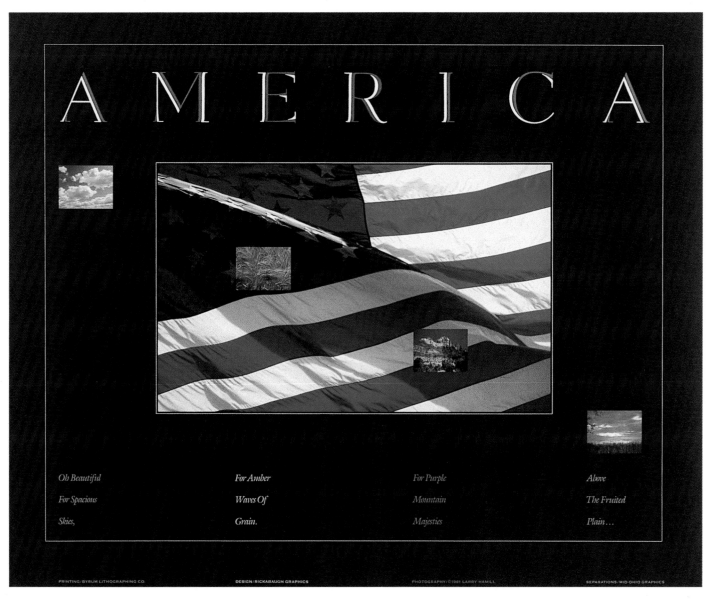

Inspired by the patriotic fervor created by the Persian Gulf war and "America the Beautiful." All services on the six-color poster, including the photography by Larry Hamill, were donated. It was sold in the firm's retail outlet, and profits were given to the U.S.O.

Direct-mail announcement for a speaking engagement of Charles S. Anderson. The firm donated their design services to client Millcraft Paper. The two-color card simulates the Anderson "look" and by using the pop-up format, grabs audience attention. The design is not as elaborate as it appears, for it is a simple die-cut and score of a single piece of paper that folds in half and glues on each side.

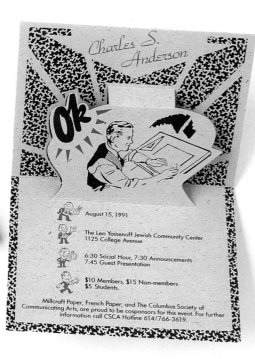

In 1990 Industrial Design Associates needed a brochure to communicate their design philosophy and display some of their creations. They commissioned the Weller Institute for the Cure of Design to do it. The result is a uniquely elegant spiral-bound booklet that manages to both impress and involve the nondesigner viewer, for as he turns the tactile pages, he sees the design changing before his eyes. As Weller explains, "The inspiration came from the original problem: Making the viewer experience and think about *design* as he handles the brochure." Some very high-quality photography, paper and printing contribute to the striking quality of the piece. Unusual materials, such as a small Mylar page and acetate pages printed with varnish, were also used. The piece was printed in three match colors and four process colors; the type and color separations were computer generated. Five hundred were printed and two hundred were bound at a cost of $7,200. Because less than half of the press run were bound, the brochure can be easily updated in the future.

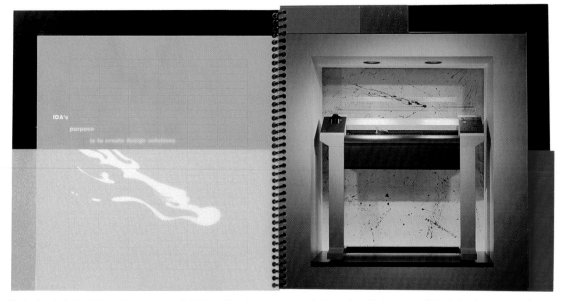

The brochure for Industrial Design Associates shares their design philosophy in an interactive fashion and lavishly shows some of their high-tech work. It is mailed to prospective clients and then followed up with a phone call, or used as a leave-behind at presentation meetings.

For these small portfolios, designer Jesse Doquilo put to use the knowledge gained in a college bookbinding class several years ago. Each is an original, slightly different from the other. They were sent to potential clients, software and hardware manufacturers, architects, vendors and the design community.

Taking a multidimensional approach to design, Studio M D strives to create work that will be interactive with its audience and make a lasting impression—through unique materials, shapes and folds; richly detailed computer illustration; and an approach in which the new and traditional often merge. High-tech meets handmade in ten small portfolio books for potential clients, parts of which are computer generated, all of which are put together by hand. Produced at a cost of five dollars apiece, each is unique as a result of the singular variety of reused materials found in each— from packaging to old blueprints.

Also unusual is the atypically shaped announcement with tucked-in business card, which proclaims the studio's change of name and ownership. The piece was successful: They kept all of their old clients and recieved thirty phone calls from potential ones.

The design, layout and type were computer generated, output to Linotronic. Three hundred were produced at a cost of $200, and the one-color, hand die-cut piece was offset printed.

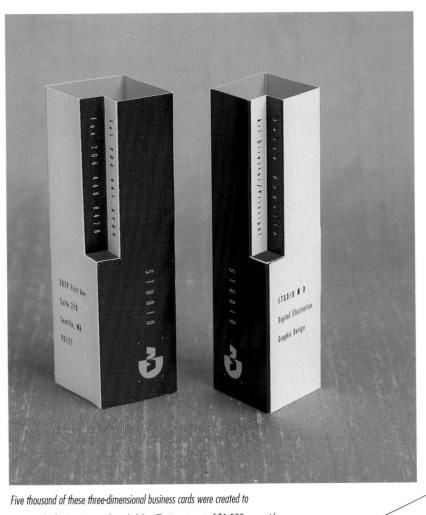

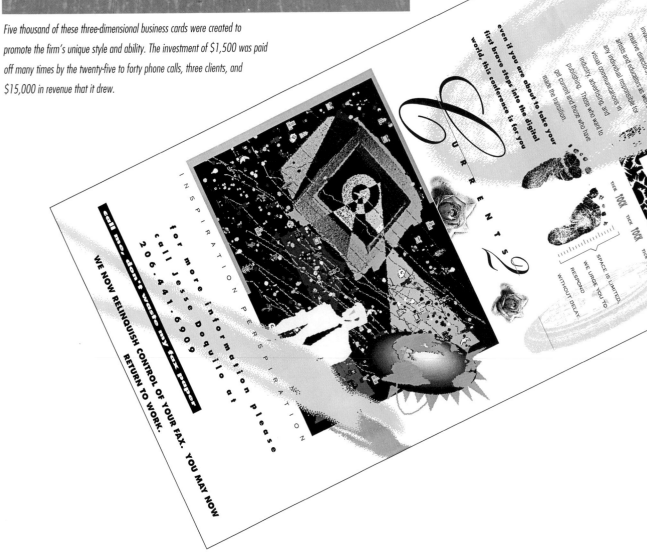

Five thousand of these three-dimensional business cards were created to promote the firm's unique style and ability. The investment of $1,500 was paid off many times by the twenty-five to forty phone calls, three clients, and $15,000 in revenue that it drew.

Because the printed promotional brochure for the computer conference was to be delivered late, this fax served as a vehicle to get the word out to the computer design community and give them enough time to respond. "We are taking control of your fax machine" was the theme, provoking the recipient to wonder what?, who? and why? The production cost was nil, while the campaign is estimated to have brought in $7,000 in profit.

Two thousand of these three-dimensional pieces were produced at a cost of $1,000 to promote the design conference sponsored by the Seattle chapter of the AIGA. Emphasizing that "with the computer, we are making breakthrough discoveries," the promotion drew one hundred fifty attendees.

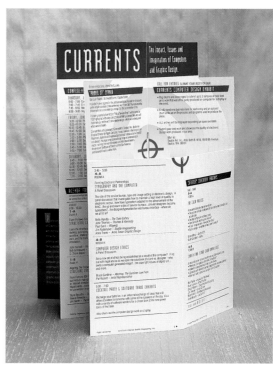

With an annual self-promotional budget of $500, Eisbrenner produced this series of business cards to introduce the studio and its offerings—illustration, design and sculpture.

Robert Louis Eisbrenner presents an eclectic mix of form, color and style in his business cards. They appear bold and heavily layered on one hand and slightly ephemeral on the other, a characteristic accentuated by the lightweight vellum they are tucked into. Inexpensive to produce, nine cards at fifty copies apiece cost $150. The pieces were laser printed in four color.

Eisbrenner's 5 ³/₄" x 8" promotional postcards, he says, were "a divine accident" that happened within one afternoon. Impressed with their color, style and intensity, he reproduced ten of each via laser printer at a cost of about $50. He received phone calls, letters, and two clients as a result. The generated revenue amounted to about $350.

Mailed to editorial art directors, designers and artist reps, these limited-edition postcards were output on a laser printer and drew two new clients.

Hien Nguyen of Pictogram Studio likes to usher in the seasons and holidays with t-shirts. "They're fashionable, people love to wear them, and every time someone receives a compliment about it, they think of us," he says happily. The above t-shirt is one of three printed as a joint project with one of the studio's retail clients. This kept the promotion's costs down considerably for the studio, at a per unit cost of less than a dollar. Many were sold in the client's stores, while the rest served as summer greetings to Pictogram's clients and friends.

The pictogram to the right was silk-screened onto t-shirts for Chinese New Year. The fact that 1991 was the "year of the ram" coincided perfectly with the last syllable of the firm's name. Seventy were created at a little over five dollars each and were distributed by hand to "existing clients, two terrific vendors, and friends."

▲ Inspired by the tropics, this t-shirt was one of three created to usher in the summer. Costs were split between Pictogram and one of the studio's retail clients, who sold the shirts in their store.

"Pictogram" is conveyed with this series of symbols, the last of which is a ram, appropriate for the Chinese New Year promotion because 1991 was the "year of the ram." The piece successfully reinforces the studio's name with clients.

While some promotional clothing trumpets and blares and makes the recipient feel like a walking billboard, Curry Design's holiday sweatshirt promotion is relaxed and unassuming. It announces the studio's new logo, which is simple and sensuous in subdued tones of gray and rust. The contemporary image, the elegant and graceful type, and the man-made and natural colors suggest the uniqueness of both Curry Design and the contrasts inherent in Los Angeles.

Conveying a slightly similar tone is the "Call for Entries" poster and follow-up card for the city's Art Directors Club. The aim, says Steve Curry, was "to create an 'only in L.A.' feel." It is achieved via historical photos and facts ("The San Diego and Ventura Freeways meet to form the busiest intersection on planet Earth," for example), and portrayal of the city's trendiness and cultural diversity. An excitement and urgency are projected as the announcement from City Hall resounds through the purple air.

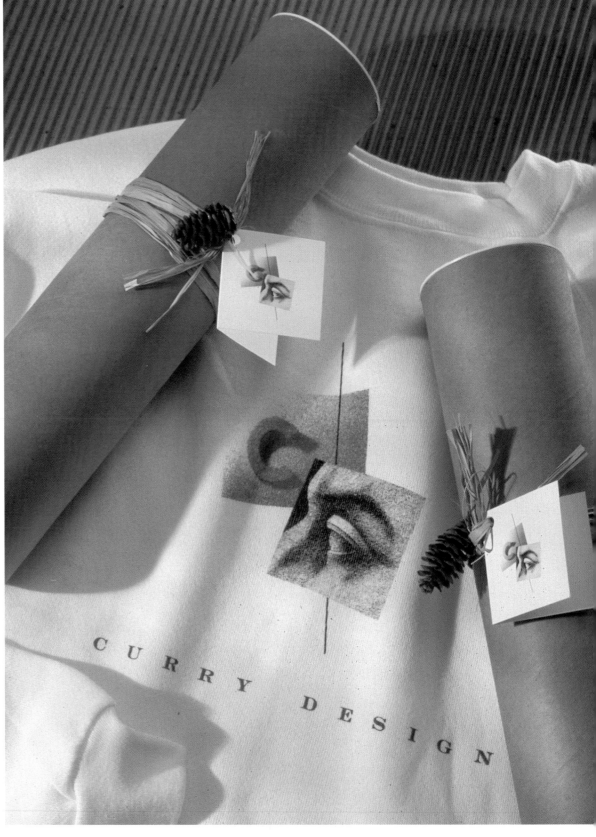

About half of Curry Design's annual self-promotional budget of $10,000 went into the production of one thousand silk-screened sweatshirts, which introduce the studio's new logo to various new businesses and clients. It spread holiday cheer with the small pinecone outside and the sprig of fresh evergreen inside the tube. The outcome was about half a dozen new jobs.

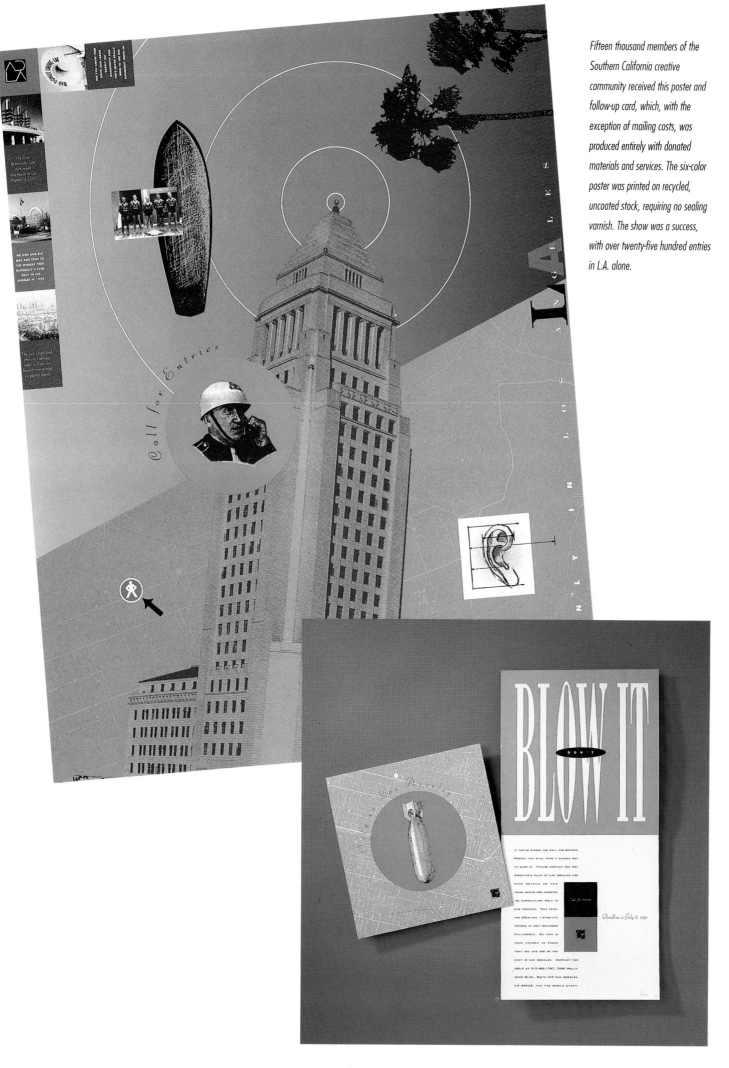

Fifteen thousand members of the Southern California creative community received this poster and follow-up card, which, with the exception of mailing costs, was produced entirely with donated materials and services. The six-color poster was printed on recycled, uncoated stock, requiring no sealing varnish. The show was a success, with over twenty-five hundred entries in L.A. alone.

To celebrate their first-year anniversary of doing business with Skil-Set/Graphix, an L.A.-based type and stat house, the studio designed the packaging for these image-setting bottles of wine and hand-delivered them to all of Skil-Set/Graphix's higher-end clients at a cost of $10 per unit. The labels and packaging were silk-screened in six color. As a consequence, a microbrewery in Dana Point called to request the design of a series of beer labels.

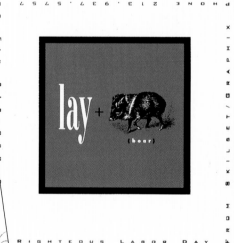

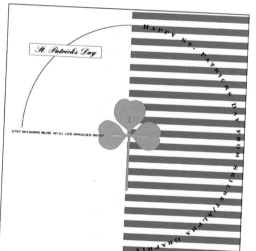

Also created for Skil-Set/Graphix were five hundred to one thousand labels per holiday, at a cost of $1,000 to $1,200. They were used for all of the company's delivery of type, stats or Lino outputs to clients. The design, layout and type of the labels were computer generated, and an in-house silk screen was used for the printing. The promotions serve as continued reinforcement of the personal, service-conscious business.

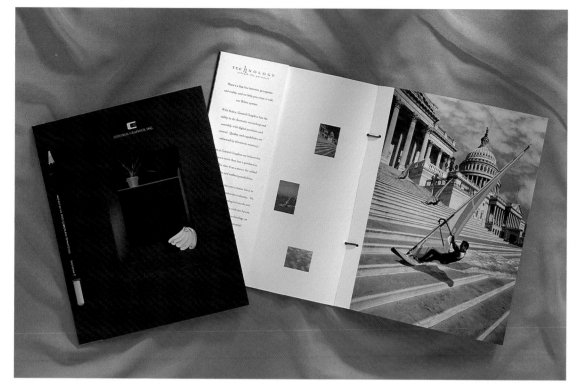

The brochure for Control Graphics, "Yes, We Have No Bananas," originates from the fruit store vendor who always had everything his customers needed. The type was computer generated, and it was offset printed in four process colors and two varnishes. To save money, uncoated signatures were run on a half size, five-color press. The photography was donated by a local photographer in credit-line trade.

The fruit store vendor of the popular 1920s song "Yes, We Have No Bananas" was committed to serving his customers and never saying "no." To Shannon Designs this seemed a smart comparison to Control Graphics, a lithographer they wished to promote as offering a complete line of traditional prepress services and excellent customer service. In addition to clever copy, the eighteen-page, 8" x 10" brochure uses specialty papers, a variety of prepress techniques, and gate-fold format to illustrate the company's proficiencies. The unique binding (of which the banana colored pencil is a part) grants the client the flexibility to add signatures as the business grows. Five thousand of the six-color sheet were produced for $90,000.

When Tannery West was opening a new retail store in Faneuil Hall in Boston, they needed announcements for the grand opening. Shannon Designs came up with this invitation, mall employee discount card and owner's manual. The design, use of color and specialty binding papers all impart the elegance and feel of fine leather.

Invitation to preferred customers, mall employee discount card and owner's manual created for the grand opening of Tannery West. Three thousand of the invitation and envelope and twenty thousand of the mall employee card were created for $17,000. Money was saved by simulating the chardonnay stock for the large-quantity, mall employee sale handout by scanning the actual paper.

Direct-mail portfolio lookalike, printed in four match and four process colors with special die-cutting. The design, layout and type were computer generated. A substantial amount of money was saved by running everything on the same press sheet at the same time. The piece was mailed to those on a corporate art buyers list, as well as those who responded to their magazine ads.

Via clever packaging and presentation, concept that relates well to their business and purpose, and continuity of graphics and color, Riordon Design creates promotions that are clear and to the point. The clever packaging of the above mailer, a response to constant portfolio viewing requests, contains inserts that relate to the firm's creative inspiration and introduce their new corporate identity. A print run of twenty-five hundred kits and two accompanying ads in *Studio Magazine* and *Corporate Source* amounted to $20,000. It resulted in twelve to fifteen new regular clients, and says Ric Riordon, "It has lead us into a different client market. The projects related to direct mail have definitely increased." In the first year he estimates the generated revenue was $150,000.

The seven-color, die-cut "Distinction Runs its Own Race" brochure came out of the studio's desire, says Riordon, "to illustrate our distinctiveness in the marketplace by using a greyhound race as a visual, the twist being revealed as the piece is opened."

The "Distinction Runs its Own Race" brochure includes thermography and cost approximately $10,000 for a print run of fifteen hundred. It was mailed to those on a corporate art buyers list. It is also used as a leave-behind at sales calls. In the first month it went out, it brought in about $25,000 in revenue.

Two thousand of these 5" x 7" promotional booklets were produced in trade to serve as a portfolio-like introduction to Frazier Design. It was sent to everyone on the studio's mailing list.

Frazier Design's brochure is a sixty-four-page booklet that presents the breadth of the studio's work simply, graciously and slightly humorously. On the back of each page's five-color image of the studio's work is a rich black varnish, which clearly reflects its opposite image back to the viewer as he turns the page. Each capability is introduced in stencil-like type on a page of glossy traffic-light yellow. A succinct and witty description of what the capability actually means runs on the other side of the spread, such as "a postage stamp reminder of the difference in you and the other guy," for "trademarks."

The brochure created for Jock McDonald is an elegant compendium of the photographer's talent at capturing—in black and white—the spirit of his subject.

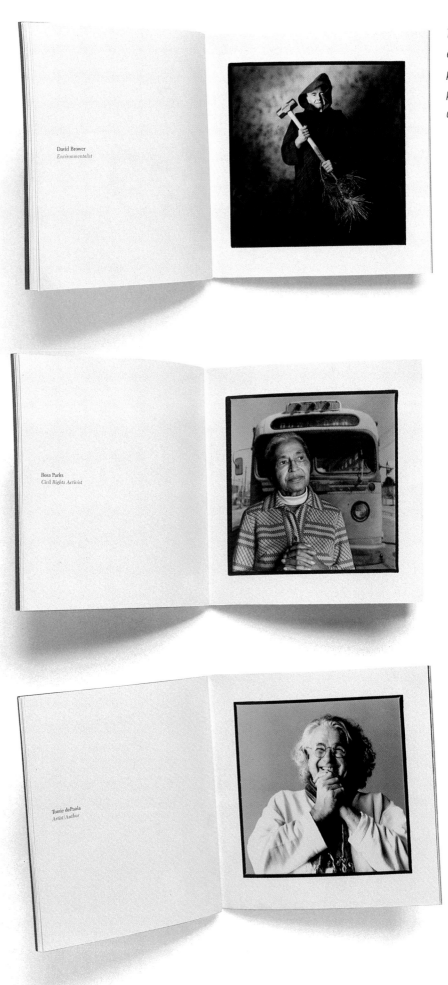

David Brower
Environmentalist

Rosa Parks
Civil Rights Activist

Tomie dePaola
Artist/Author

This six-inch perfect-bound brochure effectively promotes the work of photographer Jock McDonald by presenting his work in a clean format and letting it do the talking.

A turn-of-the-century German trade catalog was the inspiration for this direct-mail and leave-behind promotion, which drew $1,000 to $3,000 in income. Each of the four colors was printed individually on a letterpress.

"While home in bed with the flu," says Dean Bornstein, "I began sketching ideas. I think 'Tools of the Trade' evolved naturally out of the fever." Relieved that when the illness subsided, he really did have a good idea, he set about to use the promotion to most effectively display his array of services: linoleum block and wood engraving illustration, graphic design, letterpress and offset printing. Because most of the work was done by hand, the promotion was relatively inexpensive to produce at $200 for five hundred.

The alphabet promo postcard was mailed as a follow-up to show the harmonic relationship between his illustration, his capacity for bold, direct concept, and the allure of letterpress printing on imported paper. And, he says, "since most art directors love type, several tacked the card on their bulletin boards, making it a constant reminder."

Accordion-fold promotion sent to trade book and magazine art directors and design studios in New York. The close-up view of the artist's tools prompted twenty to thirty phone calls, five to ten jobs and resulted in $3,000 to $5,000 in revenue. The only thing Bornstein regrets not having done is a wider mass mailing to include small publishers and trade journals.

Tools of the Trade

**Dean Bornstein
Illustration
212-496-2695**

Pages 4 - 6 — Illustrations © Steven Guarnaccia. All pieces illustrated and designed by Steven Guarnaccia, except for Physicians Health Services Brochure (design: Steven Guarnaccia and Brent Croxton/Altman & Manly). Used by permission of Steven Guarnaccia.

Page 7 — Morla Design Holiday Card '90 © Morla Design. Art direction: Jennifer Morla; design: Jennifer Morla, Scott Drummond, Sharrie Brooks, Jeanette Aramburu. Used by permission of Morla Design.

Page 8 — Promotional brochure © Bernhardt Fudyma Design Group. Design by Bernhardt Fudyma Design Group. Used by permission of Bernhardt Fudyma Design Group.

Page 9 — "You Can't Say That" brochure © 1990 Gilbert Paper. Design by Bernhardt Fudyma Design Group. Used by permission of Gilbert Paper and Bernhardt Fudyma Design Group.

Page 10 — Stationery © 1990 Turquoise Design Inc. Artistic direction: Mark Timmings; design: Daniel Lohnes; photography: Martin Lipman; printing: Akins Printing. Used by permission of Turquoise Design Inc.

Page 11 — Arts Court brochure © 1991 Ottawa Arts Centre Foundation. Artistic direction: Mark Timmings; design: Daniel Lohnes; photography: Martin Lipman; printing: T & H Printers. Used by permission of the Ottawa Arts Centre Foundation and Turquoise Design Inc. Catalog/Brochure © 1990 Canadian Museum of Contemporary Photography. Artistic direction: Mark Timmings; design: Daniel Lohnes; printing: Dollco Printing. Used by permission of the Canadian Museum of Contemporary Photography and Turquoise Design Inc.

Pages 12 - 13 — All pieces © 1990 Ultimo Inc. Design by Ultimo Inc. Used by permission of Ultimo Inc.

Page 14 — "My Theme Song (This Week)" © 1989, 1990 Bob Tillery, © 1989, 1990 Val Tillery. Illustration and design by Bob and Val Tillery, Hungry Dog Studio. Used by permission of Bob and Val Tillery.

Page 15 — 5 x 7 promo card © 1991 Bob Tillery, © 1991 Val Tillery; illustration and design by Bob and Val Tillery, Hungry Dog Studio; used by permission of Bob and Val Tillery. "Doggone/On the Road" © 1990 Val Tillery; illustration and design by Hungry Dog Studio; used by permission of Val Tillery.

Page 16 — "Visitation" © 1991 Val Tillery; illustration and design by Val Tillery, Hungry Dog Studio; used by permission of Val Tillery. "Mini-portfolio" © 1991 Val Tillery; illustration and design by Hungry Dog Studio; used by permission of Val Tillery.

Page 17 — Emerson, Wajdowicz Studios portfolio © 1991 Emerson, Wajdowicz Studios, Inc. Design by Jurek Wajdowicz, A.D., Lisa La Rochelle and EWS design team. Used by permission of Emerson, Wajdowicz Studios, Inc.

Page 18 — White + Associates 1990 Greeting Card © White + Associates. Creative direction: Ken White; design: Trina Carter Nuovo; photography: Sherry Etheredge. Used by permission of White + Associates.

Page 19 — 1990 Mercier/Wimberg promotional calendar © Mercier/Wimberg Photography. Design firm: White + Associates. Creative direction: Ken White; design: Bob Dinetz; photography: Mark Mercier and Jim Wimberg. Used by permission of Mercier/Wimberg Photography and White + Associates.

Page 20 — Public awareness/promotional poster © North American Transplant Coordinators Organization. Design firm: White + Associates. Creative direction: Ken White. Design: Trina Carter Nuovo. Illustration: Barbara Lambase. Used by permission of NATCO and White + Associates.

Page 21 — All pieces © Jack Unruh except Triton Annual Report © Triton Energy Corporation. Design by Jack Unruh. Used by permission of Jack Unruh. Triton Annual Report used by permission of Jack Unruh and Triton Energy Corporation.

Pages 22 - 23 — All pieces © John Alcorn. Design and illustration by John Alcorn. Used by permission of John Alcorn.

Page 24 — Deck of cards and carrying case © Grafik Communications Ltd. Creative director: Judy Kirpich. Design: Melanie Bass, Gregg Glaviano, Julie Sebastianelli, Judy Kirpich. Copywriting: Jake Pollard. Illustrations: Bob James, Evangelia Philippidis. Computer production: Jennifer Johnson, Donna Whitlow. Printing: Virginia Lithograph. Electronic prepress: ALG Electronic Publishing Center. Used by permission of Grafik Communications.

Pages 24 - 25 — Holiday card © Grafik Communications Ltd. Design: Jim Jackson. Illustration: Jim Jackson, Beth Bathe, Andrea de Rose, Susan English, Ned Drew, Judy Oscer, Richard Hamilton, Melanie Bass, Claire Wolfman. Printing: Virginia Lithograph. Used by permission of Grafik Communications Ltd.

Page 25 — Gilbert Paper promotion © 1991 Gilbert Paper. Design firm: Grafik Communications Ltd. Creative direction: Judy Kirpich. Design: Melanie Bass, Gregg Glaviano. Photography: Claudio Vazquez. Air sculptures: Betsy Thurlow Shields. Printer: Virginia Lithograph. Used by permission of Gilbert Paper and Grafik Communications Ltd.

Page 26 — Poster © Systems Center, Inc. Design: Jim Jackson. Art direction: Jim Jackson, Judy Kirpich. Illustrator: Robert Goldstrom. Used by permission of Systems Center, Inc., Robert Goldstrom, and Grafik Communications Ltd.

Page 27 — SMACNA pocket folder and final announcement © Sheet Metal & Air Conditioning Contractors; design and illustration: Richard Hamilton; used by permission of SMACNA and Grafik Communications Ltd. NCMRR material © Grafik Communications Ltd.; creative direction: Judy Kirpich; art direction: Jim Jackson; design and typesetting; Julie Sebastianelli; linotronic output: Composition Systems, Inc.; printers: Haffman Press and Screen America; used by permission of NCMRR and Grafik Communications Ltd.

Page 28 — Stick Up for Kids campaign © Results. Design: Melanie Bass, Gregg Glaviano. Copywriting: Jake Pollard. Creative team: Patti Malone, Brian Hayek, Chris Greiling. Typesetting: CSI. Printing: Virginia Lithograph. Color separation: Color Masters. Diecutting: Raff Embossing and Foilcraft. Label stock: Mactac Papers. Used by permission of Grafik Communications Ltd.

Page 29 — Rick Eiber Design (RED) Stationery © Rick Eiber Design (RED). Design and photography: Rick Eiber. Used by permission of Rick Eiber.

Page 30 — L.A. Style media kit © L.A. Style Magazine. Design: Michael Brock Design. Used by permission of L.A. Style and Michael Brock Design.

Page 31 — "Canyon de Chelly" © 1991 Greg Booth. Design: Greg Booth + Associates. Used by permission of Greg Booth + Associates.

Page 32 — All pieces © 1990 Linda Scharf, except for Global ReLeaf © 1989 Linda Scharf. All pieces illustrated and lettered by Linda Scharf with additional assistance on the following pieces: Goucher College poster and catalog (art direction: Ann Lano; design: Claude Skelton); Global ReLeaf folder and poster (art direction: Jean Resteghini). Used by permission of Linda Scharf.

Page 33 — Schering Plough Employee Referral Program material © 1991 Schering Plough. Illustration: Linda Scharf. Art direction: Deborah Van Rooyen. Used by permission of Schering Plough and Linda Scharf.

Page 34 — All pieces © Gina Federico. Design by Gina Federico, Gina Federico Graphic Design. Used by permission of Gina Federico.

Page 35 — All pieces © 1991 I & Company. Design by Carol B. Neiley. Used by permission of I & Company.

Page 36 — All pieces © 1990 Pinkhaus Design Corp. Chip-A-Tree Christmas Party building banners: creative direction: Joel Fuller; art direction: Tom Sterling, Claudia DeCastro. Christmas invitation and greeting: design: Tom Sterling; art direction: Joel Fuller; Chip-A-Tree logo design: Claudia DeCastro. Used by permission of Pinkhaus Design Corp.

Page 37 — Rex Three promotional mailer © 1990 Pinkhaus Design Corp. Creative direction: Joel Fuller. Design: Lisa Ashworth, Claudia DeCastro. Art direction: Lisa Ashworth. Used by permission of Pinkhaus Design Corp.

Page 38 — Brochure © 1990 Pinkhaus Design Corp. Design, art direction: Tom Sterling. Used by permission of Pinkhaus Design Corp.

Page 39 — Nick Norwood mailer © 1989 Pinkhaus Design Corp. Creative direction: Joel Fuller. Art direction: Mark Cantor. Used by permission of Pinkhaus Design Corp.

Page 40 — Soft Cel newspaper © 1991 The Ink Tank. Design: The Ink Tank. Used by permission of The Ink Tank.

Page 41 — Christmas card 1990 © 1990 The Ink Tank. Design: Ron Barrett, Gary Baseman, R.O. Blechman, Steven Guarnaccia, Mark Marek. Used by permission of The Ink Tank.

Page 42 — *Adweek* promotion © 1989 Adweek; design: The Ink Tank; used by permission of Adweek and The Ink Tank. Music-Theatre Group invitation © 1991 The Ink Tank; design: The Ink Tank; used by permission of Adweek and The Ink Tank.

Page 43 — "Book O' Fun" © 1991 Robert de Michiell. Design and illustration: Robert de Michiell. Used by permission of Robert de Michiell. Four seasonal postcards © 1991-1992 de Michiell Illustration. Design and illustration: Robert de Michiell. Used by permission of Robert de Michiell.

Page 44 — AIGA/NY Colour Event Poster © Michael Mabry Design Inc. Design: Michael Mabry, Margie Chu. Photography: Michael Mabry. Used by permission of Michael Mabry Design Inc.

Page 45 — Strathmore Americana Promotion © Michael Mabry Design Inc. Design: Michael Mabry, Margie Chu. Agency: Keiler Advertising. Used by permission of Michael Mabry Design Inc. and Strathmore Paper Company.

Page 46 — James H. Barry promotion © The James H. Barry Company. Printing: The James H. Barry Company. Design: Michael Mabry, Margie Chu. Photography: Michael Lamotte. Writing: Marchand Marketing. Used by permission of The James H. Barry Company and Michael Mabry Design Inc.

Page 47 — The Daily Palette Calendar © 1990 The Daily Palette Group. Design: Andrea Mistretta, Jack Moore, Federico Castelluccio, Rich Grote, Nina Ovryn. Used by permission of The Daily Palette Group.

Page 48 — 1991 Calendar © Yvonne Buchanan. Design and illustration: Yvonne Buchanan. Used by permission of Yvonne Buchanan.

Page 49 — Booklet © Rebecca Chamlee. Design: Rebecca Chamlee. Used by permission of Rebecca Chamlee, Chamlee Design.

Pages 50 - 51 — All pieces © 1990 Boomerang Design. Design: Sheri Seibold of Boomerang Design. Used by permission of Boomerang Design.

Page 52 — 1991 New Year's Card © Hornall Anderson Design Works, Inc. Art direction: Jack Anderson. Design: Jack Anderson, David Bates, Julia LaPine. Illustration: David Bates. Copywriting: Pamela Mason-Davies. Photographer: Tom McMackin. Used by permission of Hornall Anderson Design Works, Inc.

Page 53 — Poster and ornaments © Hornall Anderson Design Works, Inc. Art direction: Jack Anderson, John Hornall. Design: Jack Anderson, John Hornall, Roselynne Duavit-Passion. Illustration: Scott McDougall (airbrush), Glenn Yoshiyama (calligrapher). Copywriter: Dory Toft. Photographer: Tom McMackin. Used by permission of Hornall Anderson Design Works, Inc.

Page 54 — Italia packaging © Hornall Anderson Design Works, Inc. Art direction: Jack Anderson. Design: Jack Anderson, Julia LaPine, Lian Ng. Illustration: Julia LaPine. Photography: Tom McMackin. Used by permission of Hornall Anderson Design Works, Inc.

Page 55 — Integrus announcement/invitation © Hornall Anderson Design Works, Inc; art direction: John Hornall, Luann Bice; design: Luann Bice, Paula Cox; copywriter: Terry Lawhead; illustration: Hornall Anderson Design Works; photography: Tom McMackin. Son of Heaven invitation © Hornall Anderson Design Works, Inc.; art direction: Jack Anderson; design: Jack Anderson, Julie Tanagi-Lock; illustration: Kenneth Pai (calligrapher); copywriter: Alex Glant; photography: Tom McMackin. Used by permission of Hornall Anderson Design Works, Inc.

Page 56 — 1990 Laser "Japan" calendar © Hornall Anderson Design Works, Inc. Art direction: Jack Anderson. Design: Jack Anderson, David Bates. Photography: Jim Laser. Used by permission of Hornall Anderson Design Works, Inc.

Page 57 — Moving announcement © 1990 William Reuter Design. Design by William Reuter and José Bila. Used by permission of William Reuter.

Page 58 — Moving announcement © 1992 Michael Schwab. Illustration and design by Michael Schwab. Used by permission of Michael Schwab.

Page 59 — "Join Up" poster © 1991 Michael Schwab. Design by Michael Schwab. Used by permission of Michael Schwab.

Page 60 — Gunn Design Review brochure © Gunn Associates. Design by David Lizotte, Gunn Associates. Used by permission of Gunn Associates.

Page 61 — Boston Corporate Art/Art Consulting brochure © Boston Corporate Art. Design by Gunn Associates/David Lizotte. Used by permission of Boston Corporate Art and Gunn Associates.

Page 62 — KWGC, Inc. announcement © KWGC, Inc.; design: Kay Williams; copy: Margie Bowles. KWGC, Inc. Christmas announcement © 1990 KWGC, Inc.; design: Kay Williams. All pieces: typography: Typography Plus; printing: Heritage Press. Used by permission of KWGC, Inc.

Page 63 — Christmas card © 1991 KWGC, Inc.; design: Kay Williams; candle holder: Regal Plastics; printing: Heritage Press; typography: Typography Plus. Wood baby announcement © 1991 KWGC, Inc.; design: Douglas Rogers; copy: Margie Bowles; photography: Allan Cook; printing: Premier Printing. Used by permission of KWGC, Inc.

Page 64 — Butler Blue postcards © 1991 Butler Paper. Design: Doug Rogers. Photography: Allan Cook. Copy: Doug Rogers. Printer: Buchannen Printing. Used by permission of Butler Paper and KWGC, Inc.

Page 65 — Art Directors Club flyer © Shapiro Design Associates, Inc. Design: Shapiro Design Associates, Inc. Illustration: Victor Juhász. Used by permission of Shapiro Design Associates, Inc.

Page 66 — ColorGraphics and Rusty Kay & Associates holiday gift packaging © Rusty Kay & Associates. Design: Dave Chapple. Used by permission of Rusty Kay & Associates.

Page 67 — Mitten Design Stationery © 1990 Mitten Design; design: Marianne Mitten; typesetting: Andresen Typographics; printing: Golden Dragon Printing. Mitten Design business announcement © 1990 Mitten Design; design, copy: Marianne Mitten; typesetting: Andresen Typographics; printing: Williams Lithograph. Used by permission of Mitten Design.

Pages 68 - 69 — Both pieces © Bright & Associates. Design: Bright & Associates. Used by permission of Bright & Associates.

Page 70 — Brochure © 1990 Childrens Institute for Eye Research. Design by Bright & Associates. Used by permission of the Childrens Institute for Eye Research and Bright & Associates.

Page 71 — Lisa Freeman self-promotion © 1990 by the following contributors: design: Sara Love Graphic Design; copy: Debi Key; illustration: Joseph Mahler, Susan Moore, Debbie Palen, Matthew Wawiorka; calligraphy: Juana Silcox, Joan Presslor. Used by permission of Lisa Freeman.

Page 72 — Annual Report © 1990 River City Studio, Inc.; art direction: Debra Turpin; photography: Ernie Block; copy: Terry Blakesley. T-Shirt Box © 1991 River City Studio, Inc.; design: David Butler. Used by permission of River City Studio, Inc.

Page 73 — Anniversary booklet © 1990 River City Studio, Inc.; art direction/illustration: David Butler; copy: Robin Silverman. Fish box promotion © 1991 River City Studio, Inc.; design: David Butler, Deb Turpin, Mike Bourne. Mid-America Rehabilitation Hospital promotion © 1991 River City Studio, Inc.; design: David Butler. Used by permission of River City Studio, Inc.

Pages 74 - 77 — All pieces © The Pushpin Group, Inc. Design: The Pushpin Group, Inc. Used by permission of The Pushpin Group, Inc.

Pages 78 - 79 — Southern California Lithographics poster © Lawrence Bender & Associates. Design: Lawrence Bender & Associates. Used by permission of Lawrence Bender & Associates.

Page 80 — Wedding party invitation © Mark Oldach Design. Used by permission of Mark Oldach Design.

Pages 80 - 81 — First Impression promotional materials © First Impression Printers and Lithographers. Design by Mark Oldach Design. Used by permission of First Impression Printers and Lithographers and Mark Oldach Design.

Page 81 — Active Graphics promotional material © Active Graphics. Design by Mark Oldach Design. Used by permission of Active Graphics and Mark Oldach Design.

Page 82 — Promotion © Bernard Maisner. Design and hand lettering by Bernard Maisner Hand Lettering Studio. Used by permission of Bernard Maisner Hand Lettering Studio.

Page 83 — Logo books © RBMM. Design: Brian Boyd, Tami Motley. Illustration: Robert Forsbach. Used by permission of RBMM.

Pages 84 - 85 — Crane & Co. promotions © Crane & Co. Design: Chermayeff & Geismar Inc. Used by permission of Crane & Co. and Chermayeff & Geismar Inc.

Pages 86 - 87 — All pieces © Stephen Alcorn. Artwork: Stephen Alcorn. Design: John Alcorn. Used by permission of Stephen Alcorn.

Pages 88 - 91 — All pieces © Primo Angeli Inc. Design: Primo Angeli Inc. Used by permission of Primo Angeli Inc.

Page 92 — Batik booklet © 1991 Connie Helgeson-Moen. Used by permission of Connie Helgeson-Moen.

Page 93 — Illustration book © 1990 Kathy Badonsky. Design: Kathy Badonsky. Used by permission of Kathy Badonsky.

Page 94 — Conrad portfolio © James Conrad, Artists' Representative. Used by permission of James Conrad.

Page 95 — Margo Chase Design logo poster © 1991 Margo Chase Design. Used by permission of Margo Chase Design.

Pages 96 - 97 — Self-promotional poster © 1991 Midnight Oil Studios, Inc. Creative direction: James M. Skiles; art direction: Kathryn A. Klein; design: James Timothy McGrath. MacWorld pieces © 1990 Apple Computer, Inc. Design by Midnight Oil Studios. Used by permission of Apple Computer, Inc. and Midnight Oil Studios. Stride Rite Summer Action poster © 1989 Stride Rite Corporation. Design by Midnight Oil Studios. Used by permission of Stride Rite Corporation and Midnight Oil Studios.

Page 98 — Trademarks promotion book © Webster Design Associates, Inc. Art direction: Dave Webster. Design: Todd Eby. Used by permission of Webster Design Associates, Inc.

Page 99 — IBM promotion © Webster Design Associates, Inc.; art direction: Dave Webster; design: Todd Eby. Fabric swatch business card © Webster Design Associates, Inc.; art direction and design: Dave Webster. Used by permission of Webster Design Associates, Inc.

Page 100 — AIGA party promotion © Webster Design Associates, Inc. Art direction: Dave Webster. Design: Robb Cardwell. Used by permission of Webster Design Associates, Inc.

Page 101 — Both pieces © 1991 Daniel Baxter. Design and illustration: Daniel Baxter. Used by permission of Daniel Baxter.

Page 102 — Corporate portfolio brochure © 1989 Stewart Monderer Design, Inc. Art direction: Stewart Monderer. Design: Rebecca Driscoll, Deborah Applefield. Printer: Nimrod Press. Used by permission of Stewart Monderer Design, Inc.

Page 103 — Home brochure © 1990 Stewart Monderer Design, Inc. Art direction: Stewart Monderer. Design: Robert Davison, Jane Winsor. Illustrator: Mark Matcho. Printer: The Nines. Used by permission of Stewart Monderer Design, Inc.

Page 104 — Poster © 1991 Planet Design Co. Art direction, design, illustration: Kevin Wade, Dana Lytle, Erik Johnson. Used by permission of Planet Design Co.

Page 105 — Both pieces © 1991 American Players Theatre. Credits for poster: art direction: Dana Lytle, Kevin Wade; design: Erik Johnson, Dana Lytle, Kevin Wade; illustration: Erik Johnson. Credits for summer season schedule: art direction, design: Dana Lytle, Kevin Wade; illustration: Erik Johnson. Used by permission of American Players Theatre and Planet Design Co.

Page 106 — Brochure © 1991 Arlington International Racecourse Ltd. Art direction, design: Kevin Wade, Dana Lytle. Used by permission of Arlington International Racecourse Ltd and Planet Design Co.

Page 107 — Eleanor Moore Models catalog © 1991 Eleanor Moore and Dale Stenten Studios; art direction, design: Kevin Wade, Dana Lytle; art direction/photography: Dale Stenten; used by permission of Dale Stenten Studios and Planet Design Co. The Art of the Book Conference poster © 1990 Madison Art Center; art direction, design: Dana Lytle, Kevin Wade. Used by permission of the Madison Art Center and Planet Design Co.

Page 108 — Poster © 1990 Madison Art Center. Art direction, design: Kevin Wade, Dana Lytle. Used by permission of the Madison Art Center and Planet Design Co.

Page 109 — Annual review © Dillon, Read & Co. Inc. Capabilities brochure © Dillon, Read Real Estate Inc. Both pieces designed by The Graphic Expression, Inc. Both pieces used by permission of Dillon, Read & Co. Inc. and The Graphic Expression, Inc.

Page 110 — Facing the Annual Report © 1990 Scott Hull Associates. Used by permission of Scott Hull Associates.

Page 111 — History of Design Tools © 1991 Scott Hull Associates. Used by permission of Scott Hull Associates.

Page 112 — Surviving the Creative Process © 1990 Scott Hull Associates. Greg Dearth Illustrator brochure © 1989 Scott Hull Associates. Illustration: Greg Dearth. Used by permission of Scott Hull Associates.

Page 113 — Both pieces © Gene Sasse, Inc. Design: Gene Sasse. Used by permission of Gene Sasse, Inc.

Improve Your Skills, Learn a New Technique, With These Additional Books From North Light

Graphics/Business of Art

Artist's Market: Where & How to Sell Your Art (Annual Directory) $22.95

Airbrush Action, by The Editors of Airbrush Action and Rockport Publishers $29.95 (paper)

Airbrush Artist's Library (3 books), $4.50/each

Artist's Friendly Legal Guide, by Floyd Conner, Peter Karlan, Jean Perwin & David M. Spatt $18.95 (paper)

Basic Airbrush Painting Techniques, by Judy Martin $19.95

Basic Desktop Design & Layout, by Collier & Cotton $27.95

Basic Graphic Design & Paste-Up, by Jack Warren $14.95 (paper)

The Best of Brochure Design, $49.95

The Best of Business Card Design, $34.95

Best of Colored Pencil, $24.95

The Best Medical Advertising Graphics, $59.95

The Best in Newspaper Design, $45.00

The Best of Newspaper Design Annual #14, $49.95

The Best of Neon, edited by Vilma Barr $59.95

Business & Legal Forms for Graphic Designers, by Tad Crawford $19.95 (paper)

Business and Legal Forms for Illustrators, by Tad Crawford $5.50 (paper)

CD Packaging Graphics, by Ken Pfeifer $39.95

Clip Art Series: Holidays, Animals, Food & Drink, People Doing Sports, Men, Women, Abstract & Geometric Patterns, Graphic Textures & Patterns, Graphic Borders, Spot Illustrations, Christmas, Christmas Graphics, Decorative Borders, Creative Backgrounds, Couples, People at Work, $6.95/each (paper)

COLORWORKS: The Designer's Ultimate Guide to Working with Color, by Dale Russell (5 in series) $9.95 each

Color Harmony: A Guide to Creative Color Combinations, by Hideaki Chijiiwa $15.95 (paper)

Color on Color, $34.95

Complete Airbrush & Photoretouching Manual, by Peter Owen & John Sutcliffe $24.95

The Complete Book of Caricature, by Bob Staake $18.95

The Complete Guide to Greeting Card Design & Illustration, by Eva Szela $29.95

Computer Graphics: An International Design Portfolio, by The Editors of Rockport Publishers $29.95 (paper)

Creative Director's Sourcebook, by Nick Souter and Stuart Neuman $34.95

Creative Self-Promotion on a Limited Budget, by Sally Prince Davis $19.95 (paper)

The Creative Stroke, by Richard Emery $39.95

Creative Typography, by Marion March $9.95

The Designer's Commonsense Business Book, by Barbara Ganim $24.95 (paper)

The Designer's Guide to Creating Corporate ID Systems, by Rose DeNeve $27.95

The Designer's Guide to Making Money with Your Desktop Computer, by Jack Neff $19.95 (paper)

Designing with Color, by Roy Osborne $26.95

Desktop Publisher's Easy Type Guide, by Don Dewsnap $19.95 (paper)

Dynamic Airbrush, by David Miller & James Effler $29.95

Dynamic Computer Design, by Jake Widman $26.95

Easy Type Guide for Sign Design, by Don Dewsnap $16.95 (paper)

47 Printing Headaches (and How To Avoid Them), by Linda S. Sanders $24.95 (paper)

Fresh Ideas in Corporate Identity: Logos & Their Applications, edited by Mary Cropper and Lynn Haller $29.95

Fresh Ideas In Letterhead and Business Card Design, by Diana Martin & Mary Cropper $29.95

Getting It Printed, by Mark Beach $29.95 (paper)

Getting Started as a Freelance Illustrator or Designer, by Michael Fleishman $16.95 (paper)

Getting Started in Airbrush, by D. Miller & D. Martin $22.95 (paper)

Getting Started in Computer Graphics (Revised), by Gary Olsen $27.95 (paper)

Getting the Max from Your Graphics Computer, by Lisa Walker & Steve Blount $9.95 (paper)

Graphically Speaking, by Mark Beach $29.50 (paper)

The Graphic Artist's Guide to Marketing & Self-Promotion, by Sally Prince Davis $19.95 (paper)

Graphic Artist's Guild Directory of Illustration Vol. 9, $39.95

Graphic Artist's Guild Directory of Illustration, Vol. 10, $39.95

The Graphic Designer's Basic Guide to the Macintosh, by Meyerowitz and Sanchez $19.95 (paper)

The Graphic Designer's Guide to Faster, Better, Easier Design & Production, by Poppy Evans $22.95 (paper)

Graphic Design Basics: Creating Brochures & Booklets, by Val Adkins $24.95

Graphic Design Basics: Working with Words & Pictures, by Lori Siebert & Mary Cropper $24.95

Graphic Design America, $49.95

Graphic Design: New York, by D.K. Holland, Steve Heller & Michael Beirut $49.95

The Graphic Edge, by Rick Poyner $49.95

Graphic Idea Notebook, by Jan V. White $19.95 (paper)

Great Design Using 1, 2 & 3 Colors, by Supon Design Group $39.95

Great T-Shirt Graphics, $34.95

Great Type & Lettering Designs, by David Brier $34.95

The Guild 8: The Designer's Reference Book of Artists, $34.95

The Guild 9: The Architect's Source of Artists & Artisans, $34.95

Handbook of Pricing & Ethical Guidelines, 8th edition, by The Graphic Artist's Guild $24.95 (paper)

How'd They Design & Print That?, $26.95

How to Check and Correct Color Proofs, by David Bann $27.95

How to Design Trademarks & Logos, by Murphy & Row $19.95 (paper)

How to Draw Charts & Diagrams, by Bruce Robertson $8.95

How to Find and Work with an Illustrator, by Martin Colyer $7.50

How to Get Great Type Out of Your Computer, by James Felici $22.95 (paper)

How to Make Money with Your Airbrush, by Joseph Sanchez $18.95 (paper)

How to Make Your Design Business Profitable, by Joyce Stewart $21.95 (paper)

How to Understand & Use Design & Layout, by Alan Swann $21.95 (paper)

How to Understand & Use Grids, by Alan Swann $12.95

How to Write and Illustrate Children's Books, edited by Treld Pelkey Bicknell and Felicity Trotman, $22.50

Iconopolis: A Collection of City Iconographics, $49.95

International Brand Packaging Awards, $34.95

Label Design 3, by the editors at Rockport Publishers $49.95

Label Design 4: The Best New U.S. and International Design, $49.95

Legal Guide for the Visual Artist, Revised Edition by Tad Crawford $7.50 (paper)

Letterhead & Logo Designs 2: Creating the Corporate Image, $49.95

Licensing Art & Design, by Caryn Leland $12.95 (paper)

Make It Legal, by Lee Wilson $9.50 (paper)

Making a Good Layout, by Lori Siebert & Lisa Ballard $24.95

Making Your Computer a Design & Business Partner, by Walker and Blount $8.50 (paper)

Newsletter Sourcebook, by Mark Beach $26Package Design & Brand Identity, by Coleman, LiPuma, Segal & Morrill $34.95

Papers for Printing, by Mark Beach & Ken Russon $39.50 (paper)

Point of Purchase Design Awards Annual, $49.95

Presentation Techniques for the Graphic Artist, by Jenny Mulherin $9.95

Primo Angeli: Designs for Marketing, $7.95 (paper)

Print's Best Corporate Publications, $34.95

Print's Best Illustration & Photography, $34.95

Print's Best Letterheads & Business Cards, $34.95

Print's Best Logos & Symbols 2, $34.95

Print's Best Logos & Symbols 3, $34.95

Print's Best Typography, $34.95

The Professional Designer's Guide to Marketing Your Work, by Mary Yeung $8.95

Promo 2: The Ultimate in Graphic Designer's and Illustrator's Promotion, edited by Lauri Miller $39.95

Quick Solutions to Great Layouts, by Graham Davis $24.95

Quick Solutions for Great Type Combinations, by Carole Buchanan $24.95

Restaurant Graphics: From Menus to Matchbooks, $34.95

Sign Design Gallery, $39.95

Signs & Spaces, $49.95

Shopping Bag Design, $34.95

Society of Publication Designers Annual, #28 $49.95

Starting Your Small Graphic Design Studio, by Michael Fleishman $21.95

3-Dimensional Illustrators Awards Annual Vol. 3 $59.95

3-Dimensional Illustrators Awards Annual IV, $59.95

Trademarks & Symbols of the World: Vol. IV, $24.95 (paper)

Type & Color: A Handbook of Creative Combinations, by Cook and Fleury $39.95

Type & Color 2: Blends, $24.95

Type in Place, by Richard Emery $34.95

Typewise, written & designed by Kit Hinrichs with Delphine Hirasuna $39.95

The Ultimate Portfolio, by Martha Metzdorf $32.95

Using Type Right, by Philip Brady $18.95 (paper)

The Very Best of Children's Book Illustration, from the Society of Illus. $29.95

Watercolor

Alwyn Crawshaw: A Brush With Art, by Alwyn Crawshaw $19.95

Basic Watercolor Techniques, edited by Greg Albert & Rachel Wolf $16.95 (paper)

The Complete Watercolor Book, by Wendon Blake $29.95

Fill Your Watercolors with Light and Color, by Roland Roycraft $28.95

Learn Watercolor the Edgar Whitney Way, by Ron Ranson $27.95

The New Spirit of Watercolor, by Mike Ward $21.95 (paper)

Painting Nature's Details in Watercolor, by Cathy Johnson $22.95 (paper)

Painting Nature's Peaceful Places, by Robert Reynolds with Patrick Seslar $27.95

Painting Outdoor Scenes in Watercolor, by Richard K. Kaiser $27.95

Painting Your Vision in Watercolor, by Robert A. Wade $27.95

Ron Ranson's Painting School: Watercolors, by Ron Ranson $19.95 (paper)

Splash 2: Watercolor Breakthroughs, edited by Greg Albert & Rachel Wolf $29.95

Tony Couch Watercolor Techniques, by Tony Couch $14.95 (paper)

Watercolor Painter's Solution Book, by Angela Gair $19.95 (paper)

Watercolor Painter's Pocket Palette, edited by Moira Clinch $16.95

Watercolor: Painting Smart!, by Al Stine $21.95 (paper)

Watercolor Tricks & Techniques, by Cathy Johnson $21.95 (paper)

Webb on Watercolor, by Frank Webb $22.95

The Wilcox Guide to the Best Watercolor Paints, by Michael Wilcox $24.95 (paper)

Zoltan Szabo Watercolor Techniques, by Zoltan Szabo $16.95

Other Mediums

Alwyn Crawshaw Paints on Holiday, by Alwyn Crawshaw $19.95

Alwyn Crawshaw Paints Oils, by Alwyn Crawshaw $19.95

Basic Drawing Techniques, edited by Greg Albert & Rachel Wolf $16.95 (paper)

Being an Artist, by Lew Lehrman $29.95

Blue and Yellow Don't Make Green, by Michael Wilcox $24.95

Bringing Textures to Life, by Joseph Sheppard $21.95 (paper)

Business & Legal Forms for Fine Artists, by Tad Crawford $4.95 (paper)

Paul Calle: An Artist's Journey, $65.00

Colored Pencil Drawing Techniques, by Iain Hutton-Jamieson $24.95

The Colored Pencil Pocket Palette, by Jane Strother $16.95

The Complete Acrylic Painting Book, by Wendon Blake $29.95

The Complete Colored Pencil Book, by Bernard Poulin $27.95

The Complete Guide to Screenprinting, by Brad Faine $21.95 (paper)

Complete Guide to Fashion Illustration, by Colin Barnes $11.95

The Creative Artist, by Nita Leland $22.95 (paper)

Drawing: You Can Do It, by Greg Albert $24.95

Energize Your Paintings With Color, by Lewis B. Lehrman $27.95

Enliven Your Paintings With Light, by Phil Metzger $27.95

Exploring Color, by Nita Leland $24.95 (paper)

Face to Face with Nature: The Art of John Seerey-Lester, $60.00

Handtinting Photographs, by Martin and Colbeck $29.95

Light: How to See It, How to Paint It, by Lucy Willis $19.95 (paper)

The North Light Illustrated Book of Painting Techniques, by Elizabeth Tate $29.95

Oil Painter's Pocket Palette, by Rosalind Cuthbert $16.95

Oil Painting: Develop Your Natural Ability, by Charles Sovek $29.95

Oil Painting Step by Step, by Ted Smuskiewicz $29.95

Painting More Than the Eye Can See, by Robert Wade $29.95

Painting with Acrylics, by Jenny Rodwell $19.95 (paper)

Pastel Interpretations, by Madlyn-Ann C. Woolwich, $28.95

Pastel Painter's Pocket Palette, by Rosalind Cuthbert $16.95

Pastel Painting Techniques, by Guy Roddon $19.95 (paper)

Perspective Without Pain, by Phil Metzger $19.95

Photographing Your Artwork, by Russell Hart $18.95 (paper)

The Pleasures of Painting Outdoors with John Stobart, by John Stobart $19.95 (paper)

Putting People in Your Paintings, by J. Everett Draper $19.95 (paper)

Sketching Your Favorite Subjects in Pen and Ink, by Claudia Nice $22.95

Strengthen Your Paintings With Dynamic Composition, by Frank Webb $27.95

Timeless Techniques for Better Oil Paintings, by Tom Browning $27.95

Tonal Values: How to See Them, How to Paint Them, by Angela Gair $19.95 (paper)

Welcome To My Studio: Adventures in Oil Painting with Helen Van Wyk, $24.95

To order directly from the publisher, include $3.00 postage and handling for one book, $1.00 for each additional book. Allow 30 days for delivery.

North Light Books

1507 Dana Avenue, Cincinnati, Ohio 45207

Credit card orders

Call TOLL-FREE

1-800-289-0963

Prices subject to change without notice.